Success With The Wrong Queen

British creator. American content.

Enjoy! ☺

Edited by: Oneilia Thompson
Instagram: www.instagram.com/cassiscreative
Personal Instagram: www.instagram.com/kissandrah
Facebook: www.facebook.com/cassiscreative
Facebook Group: Keeping Up With Cass The Author

Check out 'Diary of a savage' By Cassandra Dyer on Amazon kindle.

Please be warned that Cassandra Dyer is a British author, so the spellings of certain words may differ.

I began to write this novel on the 06th of February 2014, when I left home to go to university. Due to my studies, I stopped writing for a while.

Three years later, on the 4th of February 2017, I finally completed it and here we are now – you're reading my very first published novel. ☺

This story was inspired by a dream that I had. It involved my mother and an unknown male. I dreamt he was running in a marathon, then spotted my mother, and addressed her in shock.

"You came."

The main character in this novel is male. I tried my best on not to make him come across as feminine. I hope I did a good job.

This book is dedicated to:

My father for his support, wise words and encouragement. Also, for the role he's played in my life: he's always there when I need him.

My mother, for listening to my ideas, excerpts and helping with characters' names and for all the support she has given me.

My sister, my neighbour Sophia Toney, friends, family, and my readers.

1992:

Separation.

Trey and Ayisha sat on the brown, battered boxes playing amongst themselves. Every day they'd meet at the same time, at the same place, and spend the entire day together until one of their parents would call them inside. They had been best friends ever since Ayisha's family moved into the neighbourhood. Ayisha's family consisted of both loving parents: her mother, Tanya, and her father, Leroy. Her parents were madly in love and had been married for just over 11 years. Tanya cared for Ayisha and looked after their home, while Leroy worked extremely hard to provide for his family. Unlike Ayisha, Trey lived with only one parent: his mother. She was a grumpy, chubby lady who hardly ever left the house. Her daily routine consisted of sitting on her favourite sofa, smoking cigarettes, and complaining about how her life had turned out. Trey stood up and flexed his premature muscles.

"One day I'll be big and strong because of my gym," Trey said to Ayisha.

She smiled at him. "Yes, big like my dad's."

Before he could respond, Leroy had crept up behind them and scooped Ayisha up into his arms. She giggled as she enjoyed being swung around in the air like an aeroplane. Trey watched, admiring their bond, secretly wondering how it would feel to have a dad - one that cared and would do anything for him.

Leroy was a muscly, dark-skinned man, who took his health very seriously. He was well respected within the community and owned a popular gym. These were just some of the reasons Trey idolised him. Trey watched Leroy give Ayisha a piggyback then heard him say,

"Ayisha, say goodbye to Trey because we're moving to LA in the morning."

"Goodbye," Ayisha said innocently, then feeling safe and supported by her father, waved to Trey as her father walked away with her.

Trey smiled as he waved back, then went inside so he wasn't left outside by himself. In Trey's mind, he was going to see Ayisha tomorrow, as usual, but the reality was going to be very different. Leroy had finally received the papers he'd been patiently waiting for – he was going to expand his business by opening another gym, but this time in LA, which meant leaving behind their family and friends.

***

Trey closed the front door behind him and headed straight to the room he knew his mother would be in. She was sitting on her favourite sofa chair in the living room, smoking a cigarette. He fanned the air from the smoke full of toxic chemicals.

"Smoking's not good for you." He reminded her.

6

Her eyes squinted as she looked at him with eyes full of hatred. His presence always agitated her. She exhaled loudly.

"Boy, hush up with all that nonsense and stop bothering me!"

He shook his head and confessed, "Mom, I want you to see me open my gym."

Hearing Trey comment on his future gym daily always annoyed her, plus hearing him judge her for smoking angered her even more. Being true to her aggressive and short-tempered nature, she dropped her half-finished cigarette into her ashtray, then pounced up. She marched over to him and gripped him up by his neck as she spat out each word.

"You and that damn gym!"

His little hands held on her fingers, desperately trying his best to loosen her grip. Seeing Trey panic and watching the tears race down his face only encouraged her more, so she tightened her grip. Suddenly, the doorbell rang, snapping her out of kill mode. She set Trey's neck free and watched him drop to the floor. After hearing the satisfying sound of his body connecting with the carpet, she walked back over to her sofa, calmly sat down then demanded that Trey answered the door. While desperately grasping for his breath, Trey forced himself up and did as he was told. He opened the door to a tall Indian man and a short, dark-skinned woman standing in the doorway, both were smartly dressed. The lady was wearing a tight pencil skirt that matched her cream blazer. Secured onto the blazer over her tight fitted white shirt is a badge that displayed on the name Claire. Her natural, curly hair was in a tight, high puff with her curls dangling freely. Because of her hair being in a tight bun, her kind, dark brown eyes glistened, making everyone feel safe in her presence. Trey's eyes connected with the lady, as she gasped at what she saw. To her surprise, there stood a helpless young child gasping for his breath with his hands around his neck. His eyes looked bloodshed red, and he was choking uncontrollably.

Naturally, she knelt in front of him and tried her best to comfort him. She rubbed his back in a circular motion and demonstrated how to breathe correctly, inhaling and exhaling repeatedly. While Claire attended to Trey, her colleague walked around them and headed into the living room. Once he stepped in, he spotted Trey's mother smoking her cigarette, not showing a hint of remorse. He wasted no time and addressed her.

"Ms Waterhouse, we've received complaints of neglect," he paused then looked back at Trey, who was still choking, then carried on, "and from the looks of it, we can see abuse has been happening too." She grunted, refusing to say anything back. "We're here to take Trey into care," he told her. Refusing to share eye contact with him, she simply huffed, then shooed them away.

***

Claire stood over the sink rinsing a hand full of fresh vegetables preparing their dinner. Suddenly, she heard Terry enter the kitchen, which startled her.

"You scared me." She chuckled in relief. Hearing no reply, she turned around to see him pulling out a seat from under the table and sitting down. Sensing something was wrong with her husband of 13 years, she dried her hands then rushed over to him. "What's the matter?" She asked quickly.

Terry looked straight at her with a straight face. "When were you going to tell me?" She smirked, then sat next to him, knowing exactly what he meant. "Claire, it's not funny!" Terry said, referring to her smirk, then continued in an annoyed tone, "I came home to see some kid playing on **MY** PlayStation!" She rested her arms onto the table then explained passionately.

"I know, but I just couldn't help myself! You should have seen the way that poor boy was being treated. I felt so sorry for him; I just had to take him home."

Terry shook his head.

"Don't you think we should have spoken about this before you made such a huge decision?"

Claire held his hand then agreed, "I know, but he's here now, and he's the sweetest!"

***

A few months passed, and Trey adjusted to his new life. He finally has a family: a loving mother and a male figure in his life, but it wasn't how he had imagined it. Terry wasn't loving and caring like Leroy. He hardly gave Trey any attention unless they played on the PlayStation together.

As Claire prepared dinner, she listened to Terry speak about his day at work.

"They got us all together to show us the latest model that they will be releasing soon."

"Oh wow, what have they done differently this time?" Claire asked.

"They've upgraded the memory and made a slimmer version."

"So, they've made the same thing?" said Claire, summarising what she had heard.

"No, it's not the same thing, they've made a few changes to improve the previous model," Terry told her defensively before he opened his briefcase with the intent to show her the rendered model. As he reached for the print on an A3 sheet of paper, Trey came running into the kitchen excitedly, waving a piece of paper in his hand. As he panted, he called.

"Look, mom!"

"What's this?" she asked, then looked at the paper in his hand and took it off him.

"I got the best mark in the class," Trey told her proudly. He had the biggest smile on his face. Realising that he no longer had Claire's attention, Terry slammed the briefcase shut then walked out, hearing Claire continue talking to Trey.

"See, I told you! You can do anything you set your mind to."

***

Claire drove her car carefully onto their drive, then secured it with the handbrake. She got out, then helped Trey carry all the toys he had won into the house.

"That was *so* fun!" Trey said, referring to his first time going to a theme park. He loved every second of it.

"I'm glad you enjoyed yourself," Claire said proudly, until she realised Terry's car wasn't on their drive. Usually, he would be home by now, but she figured he had met up with his gaming buddies.

"I want to go back," Trey confessed, as he reluctantly closed the front door behind him.

"Well, you can, if you continue to do really well at school," Claire said, as she hung her coat up.

"I will," Trey promised, then made his way into the living room.

Upstairs, Claire entered her dark bedroom. As the lights sensed her presence, they flickered a few times before the room was well lit. She threw her phone onto their bed as she made her way over to the walk-in closet. Once the lights flickered on, she gasped and at the same exact time heard Trey call for her in shock, before he came running up the stairs into their room.

"Mom, the TV and the PlayStation's gone!"

"So, are his clothes," Claire muttered in disbelief.

"What happened?" Trey asked, puzzled, as he spotted the empty hangers. After a few seconds of thinking, Claire encouraged Trey to put the toys he won into his bedroom, then rang Terry. The first two times she tried to call him it went straight to voicemail, but the third time he answered rudely.

"What do you want?" In shock, she gasped silently, then replied.

"What, what... Terry, what's going on? Where's your stuff? Where are you?" She managed to ask only a few of the questions that tumbled around in her head.

"Don't worry about where I am Claire, just know that I'm not coming home!"

Registering what she had just heard, Claire quickly sat on the edge of their bed and asked more questions as her eyes began to weep. "Why'd you just up and leave? What did I do? I don't understand Terry, what's going on?"

He laughed then told her,

"You and that bloody boy, Claire. You both were doing my head in. Ever since you brought him home, he's been using up my stuff, eating all my food and playing on *my* PlayStation. Plus, you never seem to have time for me anymore."

"If it's attention you want then I'll give it to you, just come home and I will, I promise," she begged, forgetting her worth.

"Nah, I don't want it anymore he can have it all!" Terry said rudely.

"Terry, where is all this coming from?" To her, everything was finally perfect because she had the family she had always wanted. "I thought you wanted a family," Claire confessed.

"Claire, I never said I did, you forced it on me. Why would I want a kid? All they do is eat, make a mess and ruin marriages." Terry genuinely believed what he had just said.

"That's ridiculous! How do they?"

"They need attention 24/7," Terry said, before she interrupted him, summarising everything she had heard,

"So, you left me because of lack of attention?"

11

Terry refused to reply. It sounded pathetic, but to him, it made sense. "Terry, you're a grown-ass man, not a child. How could you get jealous over a kid? How pathetic are you? I bet you're at your mother's house right now. Have a nice life because I sure as hell will!" Claire yelled down the phone, then hung up.

***

Once Terry left, it began to feel like Trey's life was slowly repeating itself. He no longer had two parents; he was back to having one. Claire, who was once the light in his life was now a fading flame on a candle. She no longer played the loving and caring motherly role. All she did was skip work and mope around the house which Trey hated to see. At night, he would replay the day Terry left; he couldn't help but blame himself. He wondered what would have happened if he ate all his vegetables, or if he hadn't said such mean things when he was upset, would Terry still be here?

Trey entered the kitchen to see Claire slumped on the table looking emotionally drained and weak. He hopped onto the dirty counter, picked up the last clean bowl and made some cereal. He then carefully climbed down, spilling some milk as he did, then placed the bowl on the table in front of her.

"Eat," he demanded. Claire struggled to look through her puffy eyes at his kind gesture. "Eat mommy," he told her, secretly begging before he asked, "am I going to get a new mommy?"

"Why? What made you ask that?" Claire asked, intrigued to know what made him come to that conclusion. He bowed his head then told her.

"My last mom was always sad and never ate, so you came and took me away, and now you're sad…" he paused and tried his best not to cry, "I don't want a new mommy; I want you to get better," Trey said, finally confessing how he felt. Hearing him express his feelings and seeing how emotional he was getting, encouraged her to get up and wipe away his tears.

"No baby, I don't want you ever to think that," Claire said, then hugged him. "Mommy's not happy right now, but I will be, do you know why?"

"Why?" Trey asked with a frown on his face.

She held onto both of his hands and looked him straight in his eyes. "Because you make me happy."

He repeatedly nodded then pulled his hands away and pushed the cereal bowl even closer to her while saying, "eat mommy."

She smiled, then sat down in front of the cereal bowl. Trey watched her scoop up a small portion of cereal refusing to move until she ate it all. While watching her eat, he randomly confessed. "When I grow up, I don't want to be a dad."

Intrigued and shocked, she asked again. "What made you say that?"

Trey answered immediately.

"Because all they do is leave and upset their families." She looked into his eyes and could see how much he meant it. The last thing she wanted was for his perception of fathers to be negative. "Don't say that, not all dads leave. You'll be a great dad one day because you have the world's biggest heart."

He nodded but had to ask something, a question he's been dying to ask ever since Terry left. "But how can a man leave his family? Or not be there in the first place?"

She stuttered, then answered. "I don't know Trey, I guess they all have their reasons, but it doesn't make it right," Claire said still feeling broken inside. Sensing he was only going to ask even more sensitive questions, she got up, placed her bowl next to the sink then said to him, "come on let's give this house a good tidy."

2017:
Grand opening

While holding the front door half open dressed and ready to leave, Trey yelled over his shoulder. "Chyna, hurry up!" The day he had dreamt of since a young boy and worked so hard on making a reality is finally here, and as usual, Chyna was taking forever to get ready.

While admiring her perfected makeup in the mirror, she yelled back. "I'm coming, just a sec!" She then stood up and rushed over to their bed, where she had three dresses neatly placed on their duvet.

After standing there for a few more minutes waiting, Trey decided to leave the house and wait for her in the car, hoping that would encourage her to get ready even faster. He waited approximately 11 minutes before Chyna joined him. Although he was annoyed for waiting so long, seeing her all dolled up made it worth the wait. He watched her get into the car.

"You look beautiful," he told her.

She giggled flirtatiously, then replied, as she pulled out her phone and started to take some selfies.

"Why thank you, I'm red carpet ready."

Trey's Mercedes pulled up outside the gym aligning with the red carpet. He opened his door to hear some voices in the crowd mutter excitedly.

"They're here."

After getting out of the car, Trey rushed over to Chyna's side and helped her to get out. Hand in hand, they walked towards the gym while Chyna waved perfectly just as she had practised in the mirror. Spotting the pink bow in front of the gym's doors, Trey chuckled.

"A pink ribbon, really?"

Kaleel, his right-hand man, laughed loudly, proud of the prank he had successfully played. Just like Trey, Kaleel is a tall, muscly, brown skinned man, but unlike Trey, he had no beard. They both walked over to Kaleel and stood next to him outside the gym doors. Kaleel's eyes skimmed the crowd looking for any empty hands.

"Has everyone got a glass?" Noticing everyone had, he nudged Trey encouraging him to speak.

"I just want to thank everyone who came out today to support me. This has been a dream of mine for many years and now we're actually here." Trey paused, then looked over at Claire, then back into the crowd. "I'd just like to give thanks to my mom, my beautiful fiancée, and my right-hand man for believing in me and helping me to achieve this." Feeling proud of Trey and accepting his acknowledgement, they all smiled.

"So, could everyone raise their glasses," Chyna ordered. She paused, then looked deep into Trey's eyes. "This is for you baby, we love you." Chyna winked, then clinked her glass against his.

"To Trey!" They all cheered, then took a sip of their champagne. Not wanting everyone to wait around anymore, Kaleel announced that it was time to officially open the hub.

"Okay, the moment we've all been waiting for." He then picked up the oversized pair of scissors and handed it over to Trey.

He opened them and was about to cut the ribbon until Chyna suddenly stopped him.

"Wait, baby, the photographer hasn't taken our photo yet," Chyna said, then moved closer to him.

"Oh, come on!" A voice from the crowd teased. Chyna ignored the voice, then moved to the side, placed her hand on her hips, ready for the pictures to be taken.

***

Trey and Chyna led the way with the crowd following them into the reception area. Inside, everyone chatted amongst themselves until Kaleel grabbed their attention,

"Food will be served in a minute, but in the meantime, the receptionist is ready to start making any payments for gym memberships. It looks like a lot of you could do with it," Kaleel teased and tapped one of their investor's stomachs.

Trey leaned on the reception desk, absorbing it all. He looked around at the happy faces, then spotted Chyna posing for the cameras with his investors. The gym is everything he had dreamt of and worked so hard for. Although his loved ones were there, there was one person missing... Ayisha. She was the first person he told his dream to. Remembering this, he began to think of Ayisha. He wondered what she's doing right now, this second. He then began to reminisce on all the fun times they shared, and he pondered how it would have been if she was here right now. Snapping him out of his thoughts, Kaleel gently hit his shoulder.

"Congrats brother!" He then addressed Trey's distant aura, "what were you thinking about?" Kaleel couldn't understand why he wasn't living in the moment.

"I'm thinking of Ayisha. It would have been nice if she was here to see this," Trey confessed. Before Kaleel could reply, Chyna called Trey over to take some photos with her.

Kaleel laughed. "Wifey's calling you, go and enjoy yourself!"

Sleepless Night:

   While everyone else was either sleeping or out partying, Trey was wide awake lost in his thoughts. During the grand opening, the only thing he thought about was Ayisha. In the past, Trey would find himself randomly thinking about her. He would wonder what and how she's doing, then eventually she'd leave his mind.

   Trey lay on his bed relaxing, looking around the room. His eyes skimmed the walls and came across Chyna's modelling photos, then over to his dresser where he spotted his iPad. He slowly got out of bed, trying his best not to disturb Chyna, picked it up then carried it back with him into bed. He unlocked the screen, then quickly lowered the brightness, eliminating any possibilities of waking her.

   Suddenly, she tossed over. "Can't you sleep?" She asked him calmly. He nodded, locked his iPad, then placed it on the dresser next to their bed. "Come here," Chyna called, then cuddled him. "What's on your mind?"

"I'm just thinking about the gym," Trey lied, knowing it was best that way.

"Are you scared it won't succeed? or..." Chyna said, purposely not finishing her sentence to encourage him to do it for her.

"Nah it's not that, I know it'll do good. We already took on more than 50 memberships tonight, and we'll definitely get more tomorrow when we open," Trey stated. Hearing how well the gym had done, made Chyna smile.

"So, what exactly are you thinking about?" Chyna asked, stifling a yawn.

Trey shook his head.

"Never mind, I'm good now... Get your beauty sleep." She smiled, then tossed back over and closed her eyes. He moved closer to her on the bed, then whispered in her ear, "it's not like you need it anyway." Chyna grinned with her eyes closed.

"You're damn right!" she replied.

Searching:

The gym is Trey and Kaleel's second home. They'd spend every and all day there. One of the benefits of owning the gym is that they had unlimited, free usage. After spending a few hours at the gym, they worked up an appetite for some greasy food and refused to fight their temptation. After ordering their burger meals, Trey took out his MacBook which Kaleel spotted. Needing to know why Trey had brought his MacBook with them, Kaleel asked.

"What's this? Are we looking to open another gym?"

"Yeah, well no, not yet. That's not what I'm looking for." Trey replied then typed in his password.

"Alright, so what are you looking for then?" Kaleel asked. Almost immediately Trey replied.

"Ayisha." Kaleel sighed then reminded him,

"You do know you've got a girl, right? Not just a girl, a whole fiancée who is about to become your wife."

"I know, but I can't stop thinking about her. She should have been there yesterday!" Trey confessed.

"Yeah, but Chyna was," Kaleel reminded him then continued, "you do remember who your best man is right? It would be nice actually to go to a wedding." He's looking forward to attending a wedding, mainly because he's going to be in it. Plus, it's different to all the funerals he has attended.

"Don't worry, there will definitely be a wedding," Trey said, reassuring him.

Kaleel was still hesitant but wanted to be supportive. "So, what do you need me to do?"

With Trey's eyes glued onto the screen, he said to Kaleel. "We're gonna find her."

***

They spent a while hunting the internet, hoping to find her but they were having no luck. The waitress walked over, carrying their plates in each hand. She placed them down in front of them, then attempted to walk away until Kaleel asked her,

"Excuse me, if you were trying to find someone you lost contact with, what would you do?" Registering the random question in her head, she sniggered awkwardly then guessed,

"I'd check social media?" Trey responded,

"Already did that, we checked Twitter and Instagram."

"Umm," she paused, then thought, "what about Facebook?"

"Oh yeah!" Trey said then opened another tab and typed in her first name.

While eating, Kaleel helped Trey search for Ayisha on his phone. With so many Ayisha's and only the description of black hair, brown eyes and mocha skin, he scrolled down hoping he would come across someone that fitted the description.

21

"Aren't you going to eat?" Kaleel said, looking at the full plate of food in front of his friend. He glanced up to see Trey staring at the screen. "Have you found her?" Kaleel dropped his half-eaten burger and rushed over to look at Trey's screen. "Damnnn!" Kaleel blurted out as soon as he saw her picture. Surprised at her beauty, he asked, "is that Ayisha?"

"Yeah," Trey confirmed still in shock.

"I see why you can't get her off your mind," Kaleel said then started laughing. "Are you gonna message her or not? Cause if you don't, I wouldn't mind trying my luck."

The Call:

     It had been five days since Trey had contacted Ayisha. Every day he would check to see if she had read his message, but she hadn't. He would refresh her Facebook profile page daily and kept all his calls short in case she called.

     Trey was sitting on the sofa in his and Chyna's room listening to Chyna talking about her recent shopping trip. She pulled out a jewellery box from one of her many bags then opened it. She removed the diamond studs then held them up to her ears. "I just HAD to get these!"

     "Nice," Trey mumbled, with his mind elsewhere.

     "Are you sure you like them?" Chyna questioned him, then carefully placed them back into the box.

     "Mhm." He nodded, before she looked at him suspiciously.

     "Is everything okay? You don't seem like yourself." He got up quickly, then walked over and looked in some of the bags. "I'm good, it looks like you broke the bank."

"You know I did, baby. I had to go on a shopping spree because you owe me." Chyna paused, then screwed up her face in disgust as she reminisced. "I still can't believe you had me re-wearing my clothes."

He laughed, then held her close to him as he reminded her. "That was because I was saving, but there's nothing wrong with re-wearing clothes."

She pushed him away from her. "Yes, there is, and you better keep this money coming in because I can NEVER go back to living like that again." Before he could reply, his phone began to ring. He pulled it out of his pocket, then removed himself from their room as Chyna carried on unpacking.

"Yo?" Trey greeted the person on the end of the phone as he closed the door to his office behind him.

"Trey?" A female voice asked unsurely.

"Ayisha?" Trey guessed, then listened extremely carefully for an answer.

"Yeah, it's me," Ayisha confirmed before they both chuckled in relief.

"How have you been?" Trey asked.

Ayisha laughed as she realised how much his voice had changed before replying. "I've been terrific, what about you?"

"That's good to hear, and so have I," Trey said, then asked the question he'd been dreading to hear the answer to. "Are you still in Los Angeles?"

"Not at the moment, I'm actually in Houston with my parents, it's their anniversary soon," Ayisha told him.

"Oh yeah? I'm still in Houston," Trey said proudly.

"No way! I thought you would have got out the first chance you got to **open your gym**," she teased.

"Nah, I love my city, I could never leave... well seems as you're here, we could always meet up and grab something to eat if you want?" Trey offered, hoping she would agree.

"Yeah, sure I'd really like that. What time and where?" Ayisha asked, excited to reconnect with him.

***

Trey re-entered their room to see Chyna had finished unpacking and was sipping on some Chardonnay whilst checking her Snapchat. Wanting to get there as quickly as possible, he picked up his jacket and his keys without making any eye contact with her. The jingle of the keys resulted in Chyna quickly looking up from her phone and questioning him.

"Where are you going?"

"I'm gonna catch up with an old friend," Trey said, trying his best to hold back his smile.

"But what about date night?" Chyna panicked. She planned on wearing one of her new dresses, so she could take some photos and upload them onto social media.

"They're only in town for a few days. You've still got my card, use that and go out with the girls," Trey suggested, then rushed over to kiss her on the forehead.

"Fine," Chyna said, then sucked her teeth and went back on her phone.

Face to Face:

Ayisha had only been waiting for a few minutes before she spotted a handsome, bearded, muscly man enter the building who she believed to be Trey. Avoiding any embarrassment just in case it wasn't him, she kept her head low while watching him make his way over to her table from the corner of her eyes. Once their eyes met and he smiled at her, she stood up and they hugged. She greeted him as they sat down.

"Long time no see stranger." To calm her nerves, she sipped on the drink she had already ordered.

"Too long," Trey replied, then gazed at her admiring her beauty.

Ayisha rolled her eyes. "You're still cheesy, I see. You haven't changed a bit."

He laughed then replied playfully. "Well you have, you're an actual woman now."

They both laughed together until the waiter walked over and introduced himself. "Hi, I'm O'rian, I will be serving you today. Are you guys ready to make your order?"

"Yes, please," they said at the same time.

After they ordered their food, they handed the waiter their menus then looked at each other. Intrigued to know what Trey had been up to, Ayisha smiled. "So how have you been stranger? What's new with you?"

A cheeky grin grew on his face as he answered. "Well apart from opening my first gym, nothing really."

"NO WAY! Congrats!" Ayisha gasped ecstatically. "Why didn't you tell me over the phone?"

Trey laughed, enjoying her reaction then confessed,

"Cause I wanted to see your face when I told you. So now you know what I've been up to, what about you?"

She took longer than usual to respond, then told him.

"I'm a stay-at-home mom."

"You've got kids?" Trey stammered as his heart shattered into a thousand pieces.

She paused for a few seconds then confessed.

"Nah, I was joking. I work for a marketing company."

"Ahaaaa," Trey laughed, feeling relieved. "But marketing though, I would never have guessed that."

She giggled then replied sarcastically. "Opening a gym, hmm, I wouldn't have guessed that either."

Trey laughed. "It had to be done... oh yeah, how are your dad's gyms doing?"

"They're doing really well; he's opened up multiple since we moved to LA," Ayisha informed him, feeling proud of her father.

"Congrats to your old man, he's killing it!" Trey was impressed and as always inspired by Leroy.

"Yes, he is," Ayisha agreed, "but so are you! You've finally opened your first gym; there's no stopping you now."

Trey thanked her, appreciating her encouragement.

"How's your family doing?"

"They're doing good. Once we settled in, dad bought a house down here on their anniversary, and ever since then we celebrate it down here," she told him before O'rian caught her attention. Trey looked behind him, to see O'rian carrying their food over to their table.

Once they finished their meals, Ayisha suggested they visit their old neighbourhood. Trey wasn't sure at first because he hadn't been there since he left all those years ago but decided to tag along.

Once they arrived, Trey rushed out of his car and opened the door to help Ayisha get out. He then closed the door behind her and followed her to the front of the car. He watched her sit on the bonnet and decided to join her. As soon as he sat down beside her, his eyes began to wander around their old neighbourhood.

"I haven't been here since I left," Trey confessed. He looked around at the houses until his eyes landed on his old home. "I wonder how Ma's doing." Almost immediately, she looked at him, gasping under her breath. Her head tilted to the side as her eyes quizzed him.

"Didn't you hear?"

"Hear what?" Trey asked. Her mouth jittered as she looked in his curious and clueless eyes, then said,

"Your mother died about 8 years ago now." Registering what he had just heard, his head lowered, and his heart began to ache.

"Argh... it would have been nice if I had got to speak to her to tell her I forgive her," Trey confessed.

"I'm sure she knew," Ayisha said in a sympathetic tone, then rubbed his back. Trey suddenly hopped off the bonnet, not wanting to show his emotions. He quickly changed the conversation.

"You know I got adopted the same day you left, right?" She nodded her head, refusing to say anything back. She knew he was upset but understood as a man he didn't want to show it, so she decided it was time to go.

"I've got to get back now, but we can meet up tomorrow if you're free?" she asked, and he agreed.

***

After dropping Ayisha off at the shopping mall, Trey made his way straight home. He entered their room to see Chyna sitting under the covers flicking through the TV channels – waiting for him to return. He walked over to the bed and sat down effortlessly, like a zombie. Still feeling shocked from the news he had been told.

"How was it with the girls?"

"It was okay," she paused, "we just ordered some food and watched a movie at Tyanna's. How was it with... your friend?"

"It was good," Trey said quietly.

"Okay, but you still owe me! You already know Saturdays are reserved for date nights!" Chyna reminded him as she crossed her arms still clutching onto the remote. Trey nodded, then climbed out of his clothes and crawled into bed.

Trey lay there, staring at the ceiling deep in his thoughts. It still didn't feel real to him that his birth mother was no longer here. Although she wasn't the best mother in the world, he still loved her, and it killed him that he never took time out to let her know that he forgave her.

***

"Chy, are you awake?" Trey asked and listened for an answer.

"Mhm," Chyna hummed with her eyes and mouth closed.

Trey paused for a few seconds then told her.

"I found out today that my birth mom's dead... she died 8 years ago." He adjourned his response again then said, "8 years ago! I always wanted to go back and speak to her, but I never made it a priority."

Chyna's eyes suddenly shot open quickly as she sprung up. She looked at him directly in his eyes and replied. "SO? What's the problem, Trey? Claire's a great mother and that's all that matters! You already have a mother, so what if the other one's dead?" She sucked her teeth then lay back down with her back to him. She could feel him staring at her, so she said coldly, "enough talking of the past already, good night!"

Memories:

Trey looked over at his phone. He felt as though it was subliminally telling him to call Ayisha, so he did. He picked it up and rang her as he made his way into the bathroom. He looked at himself in the mirror and listened carefully, waiting to hear her voice again.

"Hello?" She answered, sounding half asleep.

"Oh, you were sleeping?" he guessed then offered, "I can call you back later if you want?"

"No, no, no," Ayisha disagreed not wanting the conversation to end, "it's just, I didn't expect you to call at... 7:58am," she teased then started to laugh.

Trey joined in the laughter for a few seconds then confessed. "I still can't believe what you told me."

Ayisha's laughing began to fade. "I know, I'm so sorry, I honestly thought you knew." He sighed heavily, unable to say anything.

As much as he wanted to speak to her, the shock was just too much. They both stayed on the phone silently for a minute until Ayisha spoke. "We can meet up later if you want?"

As soon as Trey received the address of where to meet Ayisha, he made his way straight there. He slowly drove through the open gates, along the path and parked behind a silver Jaguar that Ayisha had described. He got out and walked towards the car, then watched her get out.

"Hey," Ayisha greeted him then closed the door. "I know it's not the best of places, but I thought it would be good for you to see where your mother is buried, and you know… speak to her." Unsure of what to say, or how to act, he just nodded, then looked around at the gravestones neatly aligned. "Come," she called calmly, then linked her arm onto his and began to walk towards the gravestones. After walking past all the headstones decorated with cards, photos and flowers, Ayisha suddenly stopped once they reached the only slot that was missing a headstone. Instead, there was a rectangular block of wood in the grass engraved with her first name. Giving it a bit of character there was a bunch of flowers next to it. "Mom brought those last week. She drops some flowers off whenever she can," Ayisha told him proudly.

"It looks like it's just you lot that do," Trey stated, then stepped forward and touched the block of wood. "It's not like she was friendly with anyone in the neighbourhood anyway." Ayisha forced out a smile, refusing to say anything back. By the look on Trey's face, she could tell he was upset. He chuckled, then reminisced. "Remember that time when the old lady's dog pissed on the porch? And mom chased after him and kicked the life out of him?" She sniggered as she pictured it all over again. "That was probably the only time she ran," he concluded, then started laughing again.

***

Trey entered the living room to see it is full of excited females, empty champagne bottles and half-empty glasses that needed refilling. As she walked past him, carrying an unopened bottle of Champagne in her hand over to the girls, Tyanna greeted him,

"Hello, Trey!" Spotting Trey, Chyna got up and rushed over to him. She stood in front of him, held onto his hands and looked into his eyes. He looked past her at the magazines scattered everywhere.

"What's all this?" Trey asked.

"We're doing some wedding planning," Chyna told him. "Plus, you OWE me for missing our date night, SOOOO that means there's no budget on my dress." Chyna jumped up and down excitedly like a cheerleader, while still holding onto his hands. Not hearing anything back from him, she set his hands free then rushed over to the sofa and retrieved her iPad. "Look at Ciara's wedding dress. I want something like that," Chyna announced, as she shoved the iPad in his face.

From the sofa, Tyanna shouted.

"Hey! Don't forget about us. We have to look good too, girl, show him our dresses!" Chyna swiped across and showed him four different dresses, as the rest of the girls rushed over pointing and voicing their opinions on which dress they preferred. Trey laughed, then stepped back, refusing to get involved. He pulled out his card and handed it to Chyna.

"I'm gonna leave you girls to figure it out. Get whatever you want, baby." As they all watched Trey leave the living room, in awe, Nichole spoke first.

"Aww, I wish I had a boo like him."

Not A Secret?

Trey and Kaleel walked through the gym, past all the hardworking individuals training hard on their temples. The sound of weights connecting, and music could be heard along with the random sounds of grunting and straining from the gym users. Trey rushed over to a middle-aged man who was lifting weights smoothly.

"Nah, you can do better than that." Trey laughed then secured a pair of 20kg weights on each side. "You'll get more ladies this way," Trey added, then flexed his muscles.

"Yeah, you're right," agreed the man, before he started to lift again with a determined look on his face.

"What's got you so happy lately? Have you been getting some more than usual?" Kaleel teased Trey.

"Nah," Trey said, then told him with the biggest grin on his face. "I've been kicking it with Ayisha."

"Nah man! I've got a bad feeling about this," Kaleel warned, just before opening the door to their office. Trey walked over to his desk then sat down, still with the world's biggest grin on his face. With Ayisha still on his mind, he pulled his phone out of his pocket to see she had just sent him a text. Smiling, he unlocked his phone and read it.

Kaleel shook his head judgementally. "Look at ya, smiling at your phone like you don't have wifey at home." He then took a seat at his desk. Trey heard what Kaleel said but ignored him. He replied to the text, stood up as he placed his phone back into his pocket, then headed towards the door. "Where are you going?" Kaleel asked, as he watched.

"I'm gonna get something to eat with Ayisha," Trey replied, then re-opened the office door. Before Kaleel could begin to express his concerns about him and Ayisha reconnecting, Trey left the office and made his way to his car.

***

Trey entered the café to see Ayisha sitting down at the table sipping on some icy apple juice. Making eye contact, Ayisha greeted him.

"Hey, stranger," then slid across a pint-sized glass of apple juice. "Taste that," Ayisha ordered with a proud smile on her face.

He sat down then picked up the glass and took a sip. His smile grew even more prominent as the taste brought back some good memories. "It tastes just like the juice your mom used to give us."

"I know, right," Ayisha agreed proudly, knowing he would like it.

An hour had passed, and their plates were cleared. The whole time they laughed and reminisced on the past – the good and the bad. After tipping the waiter, they left the café and walked side by side towards Ayisha's car. Not wanting their time together to come to an end, she leaned on her car, and he did the same. They rested there for a few seconds just enjoying each other's company until Trey randomly blurted out.

"I want to do a marathon." Ayisha looked at him, intrigued, wanting to know more. "I've been thinking about it for a while now. I want to do a marathon that raises money for kids, especially those in care homes. It'll give them something to do," Trey told her passionately without blinking.

"That sounds like an excellent idea, Trey!" Ayisha said encouragingly, then leant off the car and stood in front of him. "I love how passionate you are." Trey stood up and listened to her words of encouragement. "You had a plan before, and you did it, I know you'll make this happen too!" By this time, they were both really close to each other. Trey and Ayisha's eyes connected, and their bodies began to set off signals. They both slowly leant forward, and their lips were about to connect until Trey stepped back and cleared his throat.

"I'm engaged."

Those same words echoed in her head and punched her in her chest. "Engaged," she managed to say, feeling completely weak. She cleared her throat awkwardly, then reached into her handbag, handed him a business card, then rushed into her car and sped off.

***

Trey sat at his desk continually trying to call Ayisha, but each time she ignored him. He tried one more time, and with the same result, he threw his phone onto the desk letting his frustration out. Hearing Trey's phone and the desk connect, Kaleel flinched in his seat then asked,

"Yo, what's up with you?" Annoyed, Trey sucked his teeth then told Kaleel.

"I met up with Ayisha and told her about an idea I had." Before he could finish his sentence, Kaleel interrupted him and rushed over and sat at Trey's desk.

"What idea?"

Trey ignored him then carried on. "I met up with her and told her about my idea, then we nearly kissed." Trey paused, then confessed. "God knows how much I wanted to kiss her."

Sighing heavily, Kaleel asked. "You really like her, don't you?" The room went completely silent because they both knew the answer to that question. Ever since they were little, Trey could speak to Ayisha about anything. Whereas with Chyna, most subjects are off topic. If the conversation isn't about her, or ways to spend money then she doesn't care. Trey removed the business card that Ayisha given him from his pocket, and handed it to Kaleel while he told him,

"She gave me this before she drove off." Kaleel held the card upright and skimmed it quickly with his eyes. Once he finished, he got up and walked over to Trey's side of the desk and told him to do a search for the name that is written on the card. Standing over Trey's shoulder, Kaleel watched the screen as Trey googled the name. Once the screen loaded, Kaleel recognised the face and asked. "Isn't that Ayisha?"

"Yeah, that's her and her dad," Trey said without taking his eyes off the screen.

"What type of idea was it?"

"I told her I wanted to organise a marathon that would raise money for the youth," Trey said. Kaleel smirked as he pieced everything together.

"What if she wants you to contact her dad, so you can work together?"

Meeting up:

Trey opened the office door to see Leroy and the back of a brown-skinned, middle-aged woman, with short black hair arising from his desk. They all made their way towards each other and ended up meeting in the middle of the room.

"Trey," Tanya called, then pulled him into her hug and squeezed him. "Look at you," Tanya said, before she stepped out of their embrace and admired him. "Once Leroy told me he was having a meeting with you, I just had to come down and get a good look at you." Trey smiled warmly, then heard her say, "congratulations on opening your first gym."

"Yes, congratulations," Leroy echoed, then shook Trey's hand.

"Thank you, that means a lot," Trey confessed. From a little boy, he had always idolised Leroy, so hearing those words warmed his heart. "This is my business partner, Kaleel." They all shook hands and exchanged hugs. Tanya then rushed over to the sofa, took a seat and told them all to do the same. They all sat down and began to catch up on everything, from the passing of his birth mom to being adopted, to staying in Houston, to opening his first gym. As the conversation remained around gyms, Tanya decided it was time for her to go. She got up, hugged Kaleel, then Trey straight after.

"I'll leave you all to discuss business," Tanya said, while placing her handbag over her shoulder. "I hope to see you again soon, and not in another 20 years' time."

"Definitely," Trey replied.

Once Tanya left, Leroy sat back down. "Ayisha told me you've got an idea for the community," because he needed to know more about his idea. Hearing those words caught Trey off guard. He sat there unable to move for a few seconds. He had a blank look on his face, but his mind was adding everything up. Not only did she give him Leroy's business card, which shows that she still cares, she also spoke to Leroy about his idea. Kaleel cleared his throat, snapping Trey out of his thoughts and back into the room. He looked at Kaleel then at Leroy, who now had a disinterested look on his face.

"Yeah, um, well, I thought of organising a marathon for the community. It'll give everyone a reason to come together, and the money raised will be used to build a community hub which will finally give the kids something to do." Trey paused which allowed Kaleel to add some additional information.

"Every Saturday, we have the kids over at the gym for free." Leroy nodded, silently commending their effort and commitment to the youth, as Trey continued. "They look forward to coming to the gym as they always express how bored they are. They're constantly complaining that they've nothing to do in their spare time. So, with the money raised, it will be used to fund consoles for them to play on, along with pool tables, a courtyard for them to play sports and much more."

Leroy sat their absorbing everything in until a question popped into his head. "Where will this hub be located? Will we be looking to refurbish an old building? Or would we be building one from scratch?"

Almost immediately Trey replied. "We'll be building one from scratch. I've found some land already, and I've been in contact with a few people, but we haven't met up in person to discuss it in detail yet." Kaleel looked at Trey in shock. This was the first time he was hearing about this, and he didn't like it. As Trey's business partner and right-hand man, he thought they would have discussed all the details beforehand. Trey would never have done something like this in the past, and he concluded that Ayisha was the one to blame for this new secrecy.

"Good man!" Leroy praised. "It sounds like you've been doing your research. As soon as everything is finalised come back and see me, we'll make this all happen." Leroy stood up, with Trey and Kaleel doing the same. "It was nice seeing you Trey, and I look forward to us all going into business together," Leroy said, as he shook both of their hands.

***

Trey unlocked the front door then closed it behind him. As he made his way to his office, he pulled out his phone and began to call Ayisha. Each attempt he made was unsuccessful, but he was determined to speak to her. He walked over to his desk, took a seat and tried to call her again. Before Ayisha had the opportunity to decline his call, Chyna entered his office which startled him, so he hung up.

"What are you doing home?" Trey asked, as he was under the impression he was home alone.

"We finished shopping early today," Chyna said, then sat on his lap before she complained. "There's nothing new out yet, I've got everything already! Why aren't you at the gym?"

Without hesitating, Trey answered. "I met up with the top dog of all gyms today. He's got gyms scattered all over the world. We spoke about an idea that I had, and he's agreed to work with me."

"Congrats baby, who is he? What's his name?" Chyna quizzed him, completely ignoring the most crucial part – his idea.

"His name's Leroy Clarke," Trey said, then watched her pull out her phone and type his name into Google. After a few seconds of searching, she asked,

"Is that him?" while pointing at a tall, dark-skinned, muscly man pictured standing in front of a gym. Trey nodded then confirmed,

"Yeah, that's him." Her smile grew as she began to read the article Leroy was featured in.

"Oh, gosh! Baby, he's rich! Rich, rich, rich, rich." Chyna stated the obvious.

"Yeah, I know, but I don't care about that. Look at all Leroy's accomplished. I'm just grateful that he's agreed to work with me, so I can learn from him. With him mentoring me, imagine how great I'll be," Trey said passionately. Not hearing anything he had just said, Chyna interrupted him and showed him a picture of Leroy and Tanya standing next to LL Cool J and Ayisha.

"He even knows celebrities," Chyna told him as she got even more excited, but he didn't hear her. Seeing Ayisha's face put him straight back into thinking mode. He began to picture Ayisha rushing off once he told her about Chyna. Before he could finish thinking, he felt Chyna randomly nudge him as she repeated herself. "So, what idea did you discuss with him?"

As soon as he collected his thoughts, he answered her. "We're going to be organising a marathon that will raise money to build a community hub for the kids, especially for those in care."

Hearing this agitated her. She screwed up her face as if she had just eaten something gone off. "Trey, what have I told you? Stop focusing on those silly kids and focus on your career." Before Trey could defend himself, she carried on, "baby, I know you were once in care, blah, blah, blah, but now you're no longer poor, you're rich and successful. Stop focusing on the past!"

"Exactly, I can be a role model for them. I can show them, if I can do it, so can they."

"Stop it, Trey!" Chyna yelled. "How exactly are you supposed to make money from a community hub?"

Trey sniggered in disbelief.

"It's not always about making money."

The Community Hub:

Four months had passed, and Trey's dream was finally becoming a reality. Trey, Kaleel and Leroy worked extremely hard on organising and marketing the event. It was advertised on every radio station, every billboard - it was everywhere. Everyone knew about it, and because of that, it was the talk of the town. Although Chyna hated the cause, she loved the attention. She made sure she was present whenever the cameras were around, and she never missed any public interviews. After seeking answers, Tanya informed Trey that Ayisha had flown back to Los Angeles, but he remained determined to speak to her.

"Chyna!" Trey called impatiently by the front door. He was ready and keen to get there.

"I'm coming!" Chyna yelled, as she took one final look at herself in the mirror. Loving her reflection, Chyna smiled then walked over to their bed and picked up her special edition Prada bag. She opened it, then threw her matching Prada purse, phone and lipstick inside, then closed it as she made her way over to their bedroom door.

***

The hub is surrounded by excited people chatting amongst themselves, from school kids to the athletes that participated in the marathon, to people who travelled from different cities just to attend. As the first car pulled up, the sound of chatting faded, and everyone's attention focused on it, waiting to see who it was. The presenter from Houston news rushed over and briefly interviewed Leroy and Tanya. Straight after their interview finished, Trey's car pulled up close to the reporter. Realising where she was, Chyna quickly uploaded the picture she had just taken, checked to see if any of her blue curls were out of place, took one last look at her makeup in the mirror, then winked as she said to herself,

'It's Showtime'.

The sound of cheering coming from the crowd started once they spotted Trey and Chyna get out of the car. As they make their way over to the presenter, the group began to clap and cheer even louder. Once Trey and Chyna reached the presenter, she greeted them then kindly introduced herself before they started recording. Looking straight into the camera lens, the reporter smiled. "I'm here with the man himself and his beautiful fiancée, Chyna." With a smile on her face, Chyna held onto Trey's arm then waved perfectly with her free hand, just as she had practised. "How are you feeling right now?" The reporter asked Trey, then moved the cordless microphone close to his mouth for him to talk.

"I'm feeling good. We worked extremely hard on this for just over four months, and I know you'll all like it!"

"I'm sure we will, we can't wait to see it, but I must say, four months to build a Community hub of this size is beyond impressive, how did you manage to do that?" The reporter asked, then held the microphone close to him again.

"Yeah, I know," Trey agreed, "the contractors I worked with were on it from the jump. Everyone worked so hard on making this all possible," Trey replied gratefully.

"That's great. We understand you done all of this for your love of children," the reporter said, as the kids who attended his gym screamed and chanted. She laughed, then looked back at Trey and Chyna. "Can we expect for there to be a bun in the oven any time soon?" Without hesitating, they both answered honestly. Trey agreed, but Chyna didn't. Shocked, Trey looked straight at Chyna, and the reporter gasped silently.

Focusing on her image, Chyna pulled the microphone close to her. "Well, not any time soon, but let's focus on opening these doors to the public!"

***

All eyes are focused on Trey and Leroy. As humble as Trey is, he can't help but think of Ayisha who should be here to share this experience with him, but she isn't. Throughout his speech, his eyes wandered through the crowd searching for Ayisha, praying that he would see her, but he didn't. Leroy insisted on Trey cutting the tape, so he did with Kaleel, Claire, Chyna and Tanya by his side. Once the tape was cut and the doors were finally opened, the public and camera crew followed them inside to view the hub for the first time. Trey and Kaleel made their way around the hub, speaking to everyone, being congratulated and taking photos with their supporters.

"Well done, young man," an elderly lady said to Trey as she looked up at him through her kind but tired eyes. "Your mother must be so proud of you."

Trey nodded proudly, then looked past her at a group of people taking it in turns to hug a familiar face. He stood there watching. He watched the familiar face hug Leroy then straight after hug Tanya. He can only see the back of her head, but from the look of her straight, short, black perfectly cut bob, he knew exactly who it was. Without excusing himself from his current conversation, Trey walked off and headed towards the group. With his eyes focused directly on the familiar body, he made his way over to them, moving anyone that stood in his way. Once he reached there, he gazed at the familiar face and stated the obvious.

"You came."

"Of course, I did silly," Ayisha said, with a smug look on her face. "Are you gonna just stand there staring or are you going to give me a hug?" Ayisha held out her arms. Wasting no time, he pulled her close, and they hugged tightly, holding onto each other for a little longer than usual. To them, it felt like it was just them in the room. Once they stepped out of their embrace, Ayisha congratulated him, and they began to catch up and discuss the success of his marathon. Leroy continued his conversation with his old school friend, while Tanya stood there observing Trey and Ayisha. She watched how they flirted with each other unintentionally and noticed their powerful eye connection. She smiled conclusively, understanding what was happening. Feeling her mother watching her, Ayisha looked over and spotted Tanya's smile. Before she could question her, Chyna came rushing over calling for Trey.

"Baby, come on, let's take some pictures," she ordered excitedly, as she pulled at his arm. He ignored her, then looked over at Ayisha whose mood had changed. She stood there uncomfortably avoiding eye contact with Chyna.

Tanya placed her arms around Ayisha. "Chyna sweetie, I don't believe you've met my daughter yet. Chyna meet my beautiful daughter, Ayisha." Ayisha smiled awkwardly, unsure of how Chyna was going to act because she wasn't sure if Trey had told her about them nearly kissing.

"Hi," Chyna greeted her with a massive hug because she recognised her face from the picture with LL Cool J.

Not expecting to be hugged, Ayisha forced out a smile.

"Hi, nice to meet you."

Trey stood there smiling, until he felt someone approach from behind and touch his side.

"Congratulations," Claire whispered, quiet enough for only him to hear. He turned around quickly, and they both hugged for a few seconds until he let her go. He stepped back then finally introduced Ayisha to Claire.

"Mom, this is Ayisha," Trey said, with a fulfilled look on his face. Registering the name, Claire laughed then stepped forward and gave her a warm hug. "So, you're the lovely Ayisha that Trey never stopped speaking about."

Ayisha laughed then said at the same time as Claire. "And his gym."

Realising that they both had said the same thing, they all laughed apart from Chyna who stood there giving Ayisha an evil look.

Realisation:

Throughout the ride home Trey was antisocial. The only time he spoke or made a sound was when he agreed to Chyna's non-stop blabbering and boasting. Although all his hard work had paid off, and another one of his plans had become a reality, Trey wasn't in the celebrating mood. He has only one thing on his mind, and for once, it isn't Ayisha. Chyna made her way into the living room then threw herself onto the sofa. She sighed, kicked off her heels, then rubbed her aching feet that had been in pain all day.

"I could do with a foot massage, babe." She expected him to come running and massage her feet as he would usually do.

"Not today, Chy," Trey replied quietly then removed his gold watch. In shock, she looked over and stared at him for a few seconds.

"Okay, I'll just book myself in at the spa first thing." Remaining silent, he emptied out his pockets then placed his phone and keys onto the coffee table. "I wonder when the photos will be uploaded," Chyna said, then stood up and made her way to the kitchen to get a bottle for them to celebrate. She re-entered the living room to see it is empty. Her eyes darted around the room until she heard footsteps effortlessly heading up the stairs. She rushed to the bottom of it, looked up at Trey. "Baby, where are you going?"

He sighed heavily then replied still with his back to her. "To bed."

"But why?" She asked in a confused tone. "It's just after 9, and we've got a lot of celebrating to do," Chyna said then started to twerk.

"I'm not in the mood," he replied, still with his back to her.

Chyna stopped twerking and decided to confront him,

"What do you mean you're not in the mood, Trey? You've been acting off ever since we left the hub, you were even quiet in the car, what's the problem?" Controlling his emotions, he sighed heavily but didn't reply. His mind was telling him just to carry on heading up the stairs, but his heart was telling him otherwise. He turned around slowly, composing himself before he asked her in a calm but deep tone.

"What do you mean you don't want any kids?"

She automatically turned around and rushed into the kitchen, running away from the conversation.

"Trey, I don't want to talk about it," Chyna confessed then began to pour Rosè into both wine glasses. Once she finished, she turned around to see Trey standing in the doorway looking directly at her. She turned back around and picked up the glasses. "We shouldn't be talking about this right now, we should be celebrating." She then walked over to him, attempting to hand him one of the glasses. He stepped back refusing to take the glass off and celebrate with her.

"Chyna I'm not playing with you, since when didn't you want to have kids?"

"I never said I didn't want kids." Chyna paused, then gulped down both glasses of wine, dreading the conversation they were about to have. Hearing her lie angered him some more. He stood there looking at her with hatred in his eyes. It was like he was finally seeing her for the first time.

"Chyna, do you or do you not want kids?" Trey asked. She ignored the question, rushed back over to the counter and gulped down the bottle. The more he waited, the more impatient and angrier he became. Unable to wait any more for an answer, he banged his fist on the counter and shouted, "CHYNA!"

She jumped at the sound of his voice and confessed as she bowed her head, "no." He stared at her in disgust before he heard her say quietly, "but neither do you." Before and during their relationship, Chyna had always believed they both didn't want kids. From a young age, she knew she didn't want any, and she thought he knew that.

He stood there, staring at her like she was a stranger, until something switched in his head. His jaw jittered before he blurted out, "we're done."

"You don't mean that." Those two words shot Chyna directly in her heart, and she rushed over to him.

He stepped away from her then repeated himself. "We're done."

To her, this all seemed random, but to him, everything finally made sense. She didn't know he wanted to have kids because they never got around to speaking about it. The only things they ever spoke about as a couple was his business, fashion and getting married. Somewhere along the way, he'd lost sight of who he was and what he wanted in life apart from success.

"Baby," Chyna cried as she tried her best to kiss him, but he wasn't having any of it. He stepped out of her embrace, feeling no love towards her. It was as if his feelings for her had vanished, or maybe they were never there in the first place.

"Get out," he ordered, then pointed at the kitchen door.

"Nooo," Chyna cried in disbelief.

"What? You don't want to leave? Well, let me pack for you," Trey volunteered, then marched towards the stairs with Chyna following.

***

He slid open one of her closet doors, which was full of designer suitcases and pulled out the first one he could see. He threw her Gucci suitcase onto the carpet and opened it, just as Chyna finally caught up and grabbed hold of the handle. With Trey holding tightly onto the end of the suitcase, they began to play tug of war, pulling it forwards and backwards with Chyna begging him to stop.

Trey pulled the suitcase close to him, and Chyna pulled it back. On her pull, Trey let it loose, and Chyna went jogging backwards across the room until she dropped and landed back first onto their king size bed. He opened the top drawer where her underwear was neatly organised and gathered as much as he could, then carried them over to the suitcase next to the bed where Chyna was arising. On his way, a box dropped out of the pile of clothes which caught their attention. He dropped the clothes onto the floor and raced Chyna to pick it up. Reaching it first, Trey picked up the small, white box and read the label.

'Contraception pills.'

Dinner:

Trey got out of his car and walked up the path to the front door. He knocked and waited patiently to be let in. The door opened, and there stood Claire with a calm look on her face. She opened her arms wide, and he walked straight into her hug. After hugging, Trey followed her into the kitchen, sat on the stool and watched Claire make them both some green tea. She placed his cup on a coaster in front of him, then sat down beside him. Claire got straight to the point. "So, what happened, son?"

He sighed, then told her everything. "I got so mad I kicked her out, Ma," Trey paused then looked at Claire who is silent. She shook her head with a judgmental expression on her face, disapproving his actions. Needing to know if he acted accordingly, Trey asked, "did I take it too far?"

"Son, kicking her out there and then was too far!" Claire paused. "I understand you were angry, and that's okay because we all get angry from time to time, but there are different ways to handle situations, and I raised you better than that." From hearing the disappointment in her voice, Trey's head lowered as he began to feel guilty. He listened to her carry on. "She did play an important role in your life, she supported you and helped you follow your dreams. She deserved more than a few words and then to be kicked out." Claire paused. "Yes, she should have told you she doesn't want children... as a matter of fact, both of you should have had that conversation already, and if your relationship couldn't handle that conversation... maybe you weren't ready for marriage." Each word she said Trey agreed with. She always knew what to say and never shied away from telling him when he was wrong. From the look on his face, she knew he had learnt his lesson. Refusing to waste any more time or for him to feel any worse, she changed the subject. "I'm glad I got to meet Ayisha, what a beauty." Claire smiled, knowing that would cheer him up. As expected, his mood lightened straight away upon hearing her name. Her eyes lit up as she remembered something. "Oh, are you coming to dinner?"

"What dinner?" Trey asked, with a puzzled but intrigued look on his face.

"Tanya rang about an hour after we all left." Claire paused, then watched him pull out his phone. He unlocked it to see a missed call from Tanya and 32 missed calls from Chyna.

"Ah, I missed her call," Trey informed her, just before his phone began to vibrate in his hand. They both looked at his screen to see Chyna's name appear. He looked up at Claire, subliminally asking if he should answer her call or not. Claire nodded.

"Answer it but be nice."

He answered the call to hear Chyna sound relieved. "Hey, you answered."

"Mhm," Trey replied coldly.

"Can we talk?" Chyna begged.

He looked over at Claire, who nodded. "Yeah, but it won't be until later. I'll text you once I'm free."

"Okay, thank you!" Chyna replied, quickly and gratefully.

***

Trey carefully pulled up outside of the restaurant where the valet driver is standing. The driver walks towards the car, opens the door and helps Claire get out. With Claire by his side, they both enter the restaurant and walk over to the front desk. Claire informed the front of house employee,

"Good evening, we have a table booked under the name of Leroy Clarke."

"Yes, Mr Clarke's table is just this way, please follow me." The front of house employee said, then stepped away from the desk and led the way to Leroy's table. The restaurant was perfectly decorated. The walls were a dark, warm shade of blue with black and gold patterns on. The crystal chandeliers dangled freely from the roof, letting off a dimmed yellowy light. The sound of gentle chittering and laughter could be heard, along with the jazz band and the sound of cutlery hitting the ceramic plates. Spotting Trey and Claire, Tanya stood up and waved grabbing their attention. They all greeted each other exchanging hugs, kisses, and a handshake.

"We've saved you space next to Ayisha." Tanya said. She watched Trey and Ayisha smile amongst themselves, then sat down. "Thank you for coming, on such short notice. Last night was such a success we wanted to treat you," Tanya informed them then looked directly at Claire, "plus I would love to get more acquainted. You really have raised such a fine young man." As they waited for their food to arrive, they chatted freely. They reminisced on the past and spoke about parenting until the conversation changed to Leroy opening his first gym. Unexpectedly, Chyna entered the restaurant and made her way over to Leroy's table. Her eyes are puffy and red, and her blue, curly hair was shoved into a messy bun. Her balance is off from all the alcohol she had been drinking. Chyna stumbled over her left foot, which resulted in her hip hitting the table she was passing. The sound of the cutlery dropping onto the floor caught Trey's attention.

"What the heck?" Trey muttered under his breath then pounced up from his chair.

"Trey," Chyna called then ran over to him.

"What are you doing here?" He questioned her, then looked around at all the annoyed and intrigued faces. Chyna looked around the table, through her puffy eyes and spotted the seating arrangements.

"No, what are you doing here with her? You dumped me, and you're already out playing happy families!" Chyna shouted at the top of her lungs. Ayisha sat there for a few seconds staring at Chyna in shock. Hearing that they were no longer an item was news to her. She then looked around at all the eyes that are now watching.

"Isn't it best if you take her outside?" Ayisha suggested.

"DON'T YOU DARE SPEAK TO HIM, YOU WHORE!" Chyna barked as she pointed at Ayisha. Hearing his daughter being disrespected and hating the fact that they were now the centre of attention, Leroy demanded that Trey took her outside.

Doing as he was told, Trey grabbed onto Chyna's arm and pulled her out towards the exit as she screamed and shouted. Outside, Chyna leaned against the bricked wall crying uncontrollably into her hands.

"Look at yourself! Not only have you embarrassed me, but you've also embarrassed yourself," Trey shouted, not caring who heard or saw because he was so annoyed. He had never been so embarrassed. He had also never seen her act like this before.

"Embarrassed you? You've embarrassed me, going on dates with that hoe and her family, while your fiancée's losing her mind," Chyna shouted, then charged over to him.

"It's not like that," Trey said then grabbed hold of her protecting himself. Allowing him to hold onto her, she stood there for a few seconds then tried to kiss him, but he stepped back and looked at her in disgust. "You're a mess... Chy, go home, and we'll talk later," Trey ordered. With her eyes full of hope, she sobered up quickly.

"Home, home?" He nodded, took off his blazer, placed it around her then took out his phone, preparing to order an Uber.

Decisions:

After the dinner, Trey dropped Claire off then made his way home. He opened the door and headed straight into the living room. It was empty. He then checked the kitchen to see that was empty too. Refusing to walk around the whole house looking for Chyna, he headed upstairs into the room he once shared with her. To his surprise there she was. She had just finished putting all her clothes that were left on the floor back into their correct places.

"What are you doing?"

"Hey," Chyna replied, startled, then rushed over and tried to kiss him.

"I didn't mean for you to move back in." Trey paused, then stepped away from her. "I meant for you to come back and get cleaned up."

"Oh!" Chyna sighed, feeling embarrassed. "I thought… I thought you wanted to get back together." Trey shook his head, moved away from her and sat on the end of the bed. She watched him sit down, then walked over and sat next to him.

"But why? Why don't you want to be with me anymore?"

He sighed, then slipped out of his black, smart shoes before he confessed. "You're not the one for me."

Hearing those words felt like a knife had just cut into her chest. She slumped, trying her best to hold back her tears, but she couldn't. "Stop crying!" Trey said quickly. He hated seeing Chyna cry and didn't want her to be upset, but knew he had to address this now or else he never would. "Chy, you're really not the one for me. We both want different things in life, I want kids, and you don't."

"But we never spoke about starting a family," Chyna sobbed, "so I always assumed you didn't want one."

"We never spoke about it, but from when we stopped preventing it from happening, I thought you would have clicked on… to think you were taking those pills that whole time, it makes sense to me now, cause we should have had a baby by now."

Chyna snapped. "It's my body, Trey, MINE! I decide what I do with it! Do you know what happens to a woman's body once a baby is conceived?" Chyna paused, then pointed at each finger as she reeled off the list of negatives. "The gained weight, the stretch marks, the memory loss. Our bodies are never the same!"

Trey interrupted her and said reassuringly. "I already know what happens. My job as a man and as your partner is to support you." Before Trey could finish his sentence, Chyna interrupted him and carried on with her speech jumping to conclusions.

"Just because I don't want kids, it doesn't make me less of a woman. Having a family isn't for everyone, it definitely isn't for me!"

Trey made a sour facial expression, as he disagreed with what he had just heard. He laughed.

"Who said anything about you being less of a woman? And why are you referring to other women? I'm talking about you, the woman that I saw a future and raising a family with." Chyna shouted at the top of her lungs.

"I DON'T WANT KIDS, TREY! Get that into your thick skull!" She then stood up and pointed at him, before continuing. "You're telling me you could actually see me changing nappies and staying home all day? No, I don't think so! You wanted your gym, *that* was your baby, and I helped you do that."

"I know you did," Trey said sincerely, looking up at Chyna. "I do appreciate that, but I want a kid, and you won't give me, so you gotta bounce."

Still standing, she laughed then asked him. "Where's all this coming from Trey? We were fine until that bitch entered the scene. I bet it's her that said something to you. Wait... did you sleep with that hoe?"

He laughed at her accusation, trying his best to remain calm, but hearing her disrespect Ayisha angered him even more.

"She isn't a hoe! You need to stop disrespecting her! And no, I didn't sleep with her. You're not giving me what I want so there's no point wasting any more time on you," Trey said rudely, got up and headed for her suitcase. She chased after him, snatched the suitcase, then began to pack.

"Fine! If you want me out, then I'm out!" He stood there watching her as she began to throw her stuff inside her suitcase. From how carelessly she was throwing her designer clothes inside, he knew she was enraged.

"Look, I don't want there to be any hard feelings between us."

She ignored him and carried on packing. "Chyna I really appreciate everything you've done for me; I honestly mean that..."

Before he could finish his sentence, she told him as she zipped shut her suitcase. "Good, cause I'm keeping the Porsche!"

"And that's fine! Keep the car, shoot, keep the ring, your Mac, iPad, clothes and shoes. You deserve them." Trey insisted.

Once everything was packed, Chyna dragged each suitcase along the corridor, down the stairs, along the hallway and into the Porsche refusing Trey's help. After loading everything into the car, she threw her front and back door keys at him, hopped into the car and warned him.

"You're gonna regret this!"

Bittersweet:

Usually, Trey would already be up, showered and at the gym just before 9 am, but today is different. It is 9:53 am, and Trey lay there in bed alone lost in his thoughts. This was the first time in years he had woken up to an empty bed. He could no longer playfully request breakfast in bed from Chyna, knowing she would decline and ask if she looked like a maid. He then began to reminisce about what happened last night until he started to think about Ayisha. He reached for his phone and unplugged the charger, to see the screen light up and display a picture of Chyna with a Snapchat filter on. Mentally noting to change his display picture, he unlocked it and rung Ayisha.

"Hey," Ayisha answered quickly. She had been waiting for his call but kept stopping herself from calling him just in case he was with Chyna. Trey's face lit up as he heard her voice. With a massive smile he replied.

"Hey, how are you doing pretty lady?"

"I'm doing okay... how did it go last night?"

"It went alright," Trey paused, "she moved out."

Ayisha sighed silently, secretly relieved.

"Oh wow, sorry to hear that... we can meet up and grab something to eat if you want?" To which he agreed to immediately.

***

Trey arrived first, so he decided to check his social media while he waited. Sensing a presence approaching him, he locked his phone, placed it on the table and turned around to see it was Ayisha. Trey stood up to hug her then sat back down. "How' you doing?" He watched her take off her waistcoat.

Ayisha looked straight at him and said,

"No, how are you doing? Mr newly single," as she hung her coat on the back of her chair.

Immediately Trey replied. "I'm feeling better now that I'm on a date with a cutie."

"This isn't no date Mr, this is just two **friends** meeting up to eat some good food, to mend a broken heart." She giggled.

"So, what I'm just a *friend* now?" Trey gasped as he placed his hands on his chest and pretended to be offended. She laughed for a while then picked up the menus and handed him one. After ordering their pancakes and orange juice, they spoke amongst themselves constantly laughing, until an elderly woman made her way over to their table and interrupted their conversation.

"Excuse me young man, are you Trey?" They both looked up at her and Trey nodded. "Hi, I knew I recognised you, I saw you on the news. I just wanted to take the time out to personally congratulate you on opening the community hub. It's really nice to know the young men of today have someone to look up to." She paused, looked at Ayisha in disgust judging her, and continued. "Just make sure you show them the right Godly, **faithful** path to follow." Awkwardly, Trey chuckled in shock then looked over at Ayisha who slowly lowered her head. Sensing the mood had suddenly changed, he looked back over to the woman who huffed under her breath then walked off to collect her coffee. Still in shock, Trey looked back over at Ayisha who was still sitting in the same position. Her body was slumped, and she refused to lookup or say anything. Trey watched Ayisha for a few seconds while he thought of something encouraging to say.

"I think it's about time I make it known that Chyna and I are over." She slowly looked up then looked around to see everyone's eyes are focused on her. Not only are they watching her, but she can also hear them muttering amongst themselves, about her, judging her.

"I want to go," Ayisha told Trey as she quickly got up, picked up her coat, then rushed out of the restaurant with everyone's eyes following. Trey got up, apologised to the waitress, tipped her, then chased after Ayisha. She rushed over to her car that is parked next to Trey's with her head bowed, desperately trying to hold back her tears. She had never been the teary type, but the embarrassment and gossiping about her was too much.

"What's the matter?" He asked, once he made his way over to her.

Still upset, she ignored him and wiped away her tears.

"What's the matter?" He asked again, stepped closer towards her and wiped the rest of her tears from her face. Sensing how concerned and genuine he was, resulted in her bursting out in tears. Seeing this made Trey automatically wrap his arms around her and comfort her. "Why are you crying?" Trey asked, in a confused tone.

After a few more times of asking, Ayisha stepped out of his embrace and told him. "That woman made me feel like I was one of them fast girls with no morals." Not bearing to see her upset for a second longer, he wiped away some of her tears from off her face. "Ignore her... you aren't a fast girl." He paused, then said playfully, "you're a slow girl." Ayisha couldn't help but laugh

63

at his failed attempt of a joke. They both laughed until Ayisha pushed him playfully, completely forgetting why she was upset. Still laughing, he stepped closer to her and wiped away the rest of her tears with his hand. While wiping away her tears, their eyes interlocked and they both stood still, staring at each other. Refusing to fight the urge any longer, he gently held onto her chin, and they both slowly leant forward. Their lips were so close to touching, when Trey's phone rang, stopping them. They both slumped, not appreciating being disturbed until Ayisha forced out a smile and insisted that he answer it. He pulled out his phone to see the caller ID displayed 'The Mrs' with a heart emoji next to it. From how close they were to each other, Ayisha could see the caller ID too. He looked at her to see if she minded. She nodded, then mouthed to him that she would wait in her car.

"What are you doing?" Chyna asked.

"Nothing," Trey lied, unintentionally.

"So, you're not at the gym right now?" Chyna asked firmly.

Once again, he lied unintentionally. "Yeah, I'm at the gym with Kaleel."

"Hmm, okay then," Chyna replied then hung up the phone.

He stood there for a few seconds and thought to himself *'that was a random and weird call.'* He then he began to wonder why he had just lied to her. He had always been so truthful and had never lied to her before. Not wanting to waste any more time thinking about Chyna, he placed his phone back into his pocket and walked over to Ayisha's car.

"The day's still young, you can always come back to mine if you want," he said.

***

64

"Welcome to mi casa," Trey said as he closed the door behind her. She laughed and watched him lock the front door, then followed him towards the living room. Suddenly, he stood still and muttered. "What… the… hell?" He looked at the coffee table to see it was decorated with torn up wedding magazine pieces. He then looked over to the sofa that was decorated with shredded material samples for the bridesmaids' dresses and dried up sticky alcohol poured everywhere.

"Oh my…" Ayisha muttered in shock as her eyes darted around the room. Trey did the same until he spotted his favourite picture of him and Chyna. He sighed, then slowly made his way over to it. Each step he took he could hear the sound of crushing coming from the scattered, shattered glass that was all over the floor. He bent down, picked up the photo that had fallen out of the frame then looked at it. He looked at Chyna's happy face then at his. He repeatedly blinked unsure if his eyes were deceiving him. After blinking one more time, he realised that his eyes weren't playing tricks on him and that his face had in fact been X'd out repeatedly. From the look of the absent ink and the white lines that covered his face, he concluded that it was done with a sharp object, maybe a knife? He dropped the picture back onto the floor then made his way over to the kitchen, stepping onto more glass and hearing the same crunching sounds. Ayisha followed behind and watched Trey turn the kitchen lights on. As the lights flickered on, Ayisha gasped as they revealed smashed glass everywhere. Everything that could be smashed or broken was, from their glasses to their mugs and even their ceramic plates. Still in shock, Trey looked around to further discover the walls covered with food, and even the ceiling too. He exhaled slowly, walked over to the wine cabinet and opened it to find it was empty. Every single bottle had disappeared, even his Vielle Bon Secours Ale. Seeing this angered him even more. Although he didn't drink a lot of alcohol, he cherished that bottle. It was given to him by Pierre Burke, a very wealthy and respected businessman who was also one of the investors in his gym. He stood there thinking of all the things he would do to Chyna if she were here right now until Ayisha asked while sniffing the air,

"Can you smell smoke?" Trey turned around quickly, then rushed out of the kitchen. She followed him curiously, following the smell which leads them upstairs into the bathroom. They both stood by the bathroom door and spotted what looked like Chyna's wedding dress burning. They watched the combination of red, yellow and orange flames dance out of the bathtub as the dark, black smoke travelled along the ceiling.

Official:

The fire brigade arrived and put out Chyna's highly flammable wedding dress. They informed him that there was no sign of forced entry. This meant that Chyna must have copied her original key. In addition to that, they also informed him that the dress hadn't been burning for long, which meant she was either still in the house or had left just before they had arrived. After the fire brigade left, Trey searched the whole house for Chyna but didn't find her. Knowing his neighbours had seen the bright lights from the fire trucks, Trey decided to apologise and explain what had happened. After witnessing everything that had happened, and seeing how annoyed Trey was, Ayisha decided it would be best for them to get out of the house, so she insisted that they go and visit the hub. She knew that being around the kids would cheer him up.

***

Trey's car pulled up outside of the hub, which caught Jayden's attention. Within seconds, a group of 9-15-year olds had come rushing out screaming and chanting. Seeing all the happy and excited faces lightened Trey's mood drastically. Trey and Ayisha got out of the car and made their way into the hub. As they did this, the children followed.

"Trey, verse me?" Taylor said, as he picked up both PS4 pads and handed him one.

"Looks like you want your ass beat." Trey answered playfully. He accepted the controller that was being held in his direction.

"Aha." Taylor laughed sarcastically.

"Loser does 30 pushups." His friend suggested.

They all agreed energetically and threw themselves onto the sofa, ready to watch the game.

"Trey, who's your pretty friend?" Kameel asked then winked at Ayisha. She laughed then looked at Trey. They sat there staring at each other for a few seconds until he smirked.

"That's my new lady." Trey told them proudly.

"Wait, what happened to Chyna and her fine ass?" Zain asked. Suddenly the room went quiet. The only thing that could be heard was the intro music coming from the console. All eyes were glued onto Trey, even Ayisha's. He looked around at all their intrigued eyes then answered.

"I got rid of her. She wasn't the right one for me." He paused, then thought he'd take the opportunity to give them some wise words. "When you all start dating, make sure you're with someone you can be yourself with, and make sure she isn't one of the crazy ones!" Ayisha smiled proudly and watched him finish setting up their game.

"I'd still tap that ass." Kayden said, smirking.

***

All eyes, except Ayisha's and Kendrick's were glued to the TV screen. Kendrick was scrolling down his timeline and spotted something that resulted in him bursting out into uncontrollable laughter.

"Trey, have you seen what your ex' put on Insta?" Kendrick asked, clutching tightly onto his phone. Intrigued, Trey paused the game and they all pulled out their phones to check their timelines.

"No way!" Jonathan sniggered and read the caption out loud. "You really think you can break a bad bitch's heart and get away with it?" Trey shook his head in disbelief then turned his phone around to show Ayisha the video Chyna had uploaded. It was a short clip of her setting her wedding dress on fire.

"She's crazy yo," Ray stated, and they all started to laugh. All except Trey and Ayisha.

"She really tried to burn your house down?" Kendrick asked in disbelief.

"The crazy ones are the best." Kayden said.

A few minutes had passed, and everyone was still glued to their phones. They were all enjoying the entertainment and were constantly refreshing the page, reading the recent comments and waiting for something new to be posted. Suddenly, Trey stood up with his eyes glued to his phone, mumbling under his breath.

"What's the matter?" A concerned Ayisha asked.

Before he could reply, the sound of glass shattering travelled through the whole building catching everyone's attention. Without hesitating, Trey dropped his phone and darted out of the hub towards his car, where he saw Chyna and Tyanna circling it clutching onto baseball bats.

"You want to break my best friend's heart and act like everything's fine!" Tyanna yelled, then whacked her bat on his bonnet, leaving a small dent.

"Stop it!" Ayisha proclaimed, then rushed over to stand by Trey's side. He stood there helplessly watching. It took everything in him to not run up to them, and deal with them how he would if they were males, but Claire had raised him better than that. Within seconds, the kids had also come running outside. They started jumping up and down and shouting after Chyna and Tyanna. With the kids now outside watching, it only reinforced to Trey the fact that he had to handle this professionally. He stepped forward slowly and spoke directly to Chyna.

"Be careful, there are kids around."

Feeling agitated Chyna shouted. "Does it look like I give a damn about those little shits?" then smashed another one of his windows. Kameel laughed loudly over the sound of the glass particles landing then shouted. "Hit yourself in the head instead, it might just knock the crazy out of you!"

They all started laughing, which angered Chyna even more. She gripped the bat tighter and charged towards the kids. Finding it hysterical, they all rushed back towards the hub as Ayisha stepped forward and pushed her, acting like a barrier. Chyna stumbled back uncontrollably and tried her best not to fall.

"BITCH!" Tyanna shouted, then charged towards Ayisha.

"GET IN!" Trey shouted at the kids, then stepped in front of Ayisha, shielding her.

Taking it all back:

The sound of a gentle knock on the door caught Trey's attention. He rushed out of Ayisha's bathroom that's attached to her room to answer the door. He opened it to see the Clarke's maid holding the first aid box that he had requested. He took the box, thanked her then reminded her. "Remember not to say anything to Mr or Mrs Clarke." She nodded, turned away and headed back downstairs.

He re-entered the bathroom to see Ayisha still washing the blood off her weeping fists. He rested the box on the sink next to her and pulled out a plaster.

"I can't believe that bitch!" Ayisha yelled.

After running up from behind, Chyna managed to hit Ayisha and they all started pushing and shoving and swinging their fists until Trey managed to separate them.

"Who goes for kids, really?" Ayisha asked in disbelief. Refusing to say anything, Trey picked up one of the neatly stacked hand towels and started to dry her hands gently. Feeling the fabric from the towel touch her open wounds, she hissed then retrieved her hand from his grip. Still silent, he reached for a plaster and started to dress one of her many wounds. "She's out of control Trey, she needs to be stopped!" Ayisha said firmly.

He sucked his teeth then threw the empty packaging in the bin, still refusing to say anything.

"Trey?" Ayisha waited for him to answer.

"Mhm, I'll speak to her," he replied in a low and distant tone.

"Talk? Just talk, Trey? SHE'S OUT OF CONTROL! She smashed everything in your house, then tried to burn it down. You're forgetting that she just wrecked your car windows, *tried to attack the kids* and then drove away, acting like nothing happened," Ayisha reminded him hoping this would make him realise how serious this situation is.

"WHAT AM I SUPPOSED TO DO?" Trey finally yelled.

"You see the Porsche she drives? TAKE IT BACK," she paused, "Trey, you're so blinded by her that you haven't realised how serious this has gotten. What would have happened if she hit one of the kids? I guarantee their parents wouldn't have taken that well and who knows, it might have even ended in getting the hub closed," Ayisha told him. "Trey, you're not together anymore, stop protecting her. She's never going to learn if she doesn't get a taste of her own medicine." He stood there for a few seconds absorbing everything that he had just heard. He knew Chyna loved to get her way, which was one of the many things he loved about her but hearing the list of things she had done finally made him realise she had gone too far. He took his phone out of his pocket and walked out of the bathroom while dialling his car insurance.

He sat down on the sofa just in time to hear the voice on the other side answer.

"What's good, boss man? You calling to insure another Porsche?"

Immediately Trey replied. "Not this time my brother, I'm actually calling for a favour."

"What's up? What do you need? Anything, man," Quan asked, eager to help.

"I kicked Chyna out because she's been acting up and I need to shake her up a bit."

"OH YEAH! I heard about that, she's been sending for you all over social media, what did you do to her?" Quan laughed.

"She's acting up cause I'm back with my old girl."

"Okay, I see," Quan replied.

"Mm, so I need you to get my Porsche back for me."

"Trey, you know I can't do that," Quan told him quickly.

"I'm sure there's something you can do, plus you owe me anyway," Trey reminded him.

Quan stuttered on the other end of the line, thinking of a way he could help.

"Alright, I got you. I'll get one of my boys to get it for you. Do you know where it is?" Quan asked.

"Nah, I don't have time to be tracking anything."

"Aha, I know you're a busy man. I'll get someone to track your car, once we've found it, I'll hit you back, alright?"

"Nice one," Trey said gratefully, then ended the call.

As soon as the call ended, Ayisha walked in and sat down next to him. "What about her card?" Ayisha asked while leaning forward to grab the TV remote.

"Oh yeah, I forgot about her bank account."

"Bank account?" Ayisha repeated curiously.

"Yeah, she's got my card, and I opened an account for her."

"What for?" Ayisha questioned him in disbelief.

"I'd put money in that bank account weekly," Trey mumbled, avoiding looking at her.

"No wonder she's acting like this, you've been treating her like some kind of princess," Ayisha said as she shook her head still in disbelief.

"Shut it down now, Trey!" Trey unlocked his phone to feel it vibrate in his hand then display Quan's name on the screen.

"Hello?" Trey answered, then listened for a reply.

"One of my boys found your Porsche, and he's on his way to get it. Where about are you?" Quan asked.

"I'm at my girl's right now but get them to drop it off at mine," Trey said.

"Alright, I got you," Quan said quickly. Trey thanked him, then ended the call. Before he could rest his phone back down, Ayisha commanded with a straight face.

"Now call the bank."

***

Trey and Ayisha were cuddling on the sofa watching an episode of My Wife and Kids. Throughout the whole episode they couldn't help but laugh. Not only did they find the episode hilarious, they also felt free. Free to enjoy each other's company without feeling guilty. They both laughed loudly together until Trey's phone began to ring. Ayisha sat up from laying on his chest, and they both looked at his phone. Expecting the worst, Trey answered rudely.

"What do you want?"

To his surprise, Chyna called in a confused tone, "Trey?" His head jerked in shock because he wasn't expecting for her to sound so calm. Chyna carried on, "I tried to pre-order the new iPhone, but it said my card was declined?" He sat for a few seconds baffled at how calm she sounded. It seemed like she was oblivious to what was going on.

"I cancelled your card," Trey told her coldly.

"What! Why would you do that? That's so random."

74

"It's not random Chy, you've been acting up plus we're not together, so you aren't going to be living off me anymore."

"But how am I gonna pay for it?" Chyna asked, utterly missing the point.

"I don't know, you'll figure it out." Trey said, laughing.

Chyna sat there just breathing down the phone in disbelief. The more she thought about it, the angrier she became. "Fine then, you dumb fuck!" Chyna paused then started to laugh. "You've made the biggest mistake of your life downgrading for that hoe, I bet she's behind this, trying to live off my money!" Chyna shouted before ending the call.

As he locked his phone he sniggered, then looked at Ayisha and finally laughed out loud in disbelief.

"What did she say?" Ayisha asked without blinking.

"I think she has no clue what's going on right now."

"That poor girl," Ayisha tutted while shaking her head, "she's beauty without a brain."

"I guess that's the type of women I like," Trey replied with a smug look on his face. Ayisha gasped in shock then playfully nudged him. They both began to play fight on the sofa until Trey's phone began to ring. They both paused and looked at it.

"Hello?" Trey answered then pressed the speaker option.

"TREY! … TELL THIS STUPID MAN THIS IS MY CAR!" They both heard Chyna shout down the phone.

Disagreeing with her, Trey reminded her bluntly. "It's not, it belongs to me."

"Yeah, but you bought it for me, so tell this idiot to stop! Stop!" Chyna commanded. Before he could reply, they both heard Chyna shout and wrestle with the driver trying her best to stop him.

"Chyna," Trey called and listened for a reply, but there wasn't one, so he tried again, "Chyna!"

"Trey, everything's just going wrong today," Chyna said as she began to whine, "my card stops working and then... they take my... wait... did you do this?" Trey can hear the hurt and shock in her voice, which made him feel bad until his eyes connected with Ayisha's, and she stared at him evilly.

"Yeah... yeah, I did." He paused, then cleared his throat. "Chy it's over, you won't be living off me anymore."

"But why the Porsche?" Chyna whined. "Trey, not the Porsche, you know I love that car."

"I honestly don't give a fuck," Trey replied, coldly.

She stuttered and repeatedly sighed, desperately thinking of the right words to say.

"But, but... I'm sorry!" she begged, "baby, let's talk, you know we can work this out, this has gone way too far. I miss you."

Ayisha laughed then shouted at the phone. "You don't miss him, stop kidding yourself. You don't even love him; you love the lifestyle. Good luck catching the bus from now on, bitch." She then stretched over and ended the call.

"Well, damn!" Trey laughed, then reached forward and kissed her, finding her fiery side attractive. They both sat there kissing for a few seconds until Trey's phone rang again.

"Hello?" He answered, unsure of who is on the other end.

"Yo, is this Trey?" A male with a deep voice asked.

"Yeah, who's this?" Trey said, defensively.

"I'm one of Quan's boys. I've got your Porsche, but I'm going to be real with you, shorty was talking crazy. She was on about if she can't have it no one can," the driver paused, "then she ran inside and brought a bat out and tried to smash the windows."

"Did she break any?" Trey asked fearing the answer.

"Nah, I didn't let her, but I think it's best if I don't drop it off at yours, there's no telling what she might do. She reminds me of my old girl, she popped all of my tires and egged my car."

"Damn I hear you. I'm going to send you the address to where I'm at now, just drop it off here," Trey said, then ended the call and sent him the address.

Too far:

The sound of a horn travelled through the air and caught Ayisha's attention. She sat up straight then tapped Trey's stomach.

"I think that's him," Ayisha said.

Trey removed his arm from around her, got up and made his way over to the window. Spotting the tow truck with his Porsche secured at the back, Trey turned around to face Ayisha. "Yeah, that's him." He watched her nod then made his way downstairs to let him in through the electric gates. Trey thanked the driver then watched him lower the Porsche from the back of the tow truck.

"It's nothing," he replied, then decided to give him a warning. "My old girl was just like yours, and in all honesty, your girl's not done yet. If you haven't already, then I suggest you insure everything ASAP!"

"I hear you, bro," Trey said gratefully, then took out his wallet and handed him $100.

"Nah, I'm good," The driver said, as he shook his head, refusing the money.

"Just take it, I got you." Trey insisted. After going back and forth a few more times, he finally gave in and took the money from Trey just as Ayisha joined them outside.

"Hey!" She greeted the driver with a warm smile, then stood next to Trey and held his hand.

"Hey, I see why your old girl's mad, she's beautiful."

"Aww thank you," Ayisha giggled, "and thanks for looking out for him," Ayisha said, before she took out $100 and attempted to give him.

"No problem, but I've already been paid," the driver informed her.

"I know, and this is your tip!" Ayisha said, as she grabbed his hand, placed the money on his palm and folded his fingers over the dough.

They both watched as the driver drove along the path, then through the electric gates that closed behind him. Ayisha then focused her attention on Trey.

"Aww, he was lovely... I'm hungry, should we order food?"

"You can, but I'm gonna head over to the gym," Trey said, then kissed her on her forehead.

"Aww okay, message me when you're there." Ayisha watched him get into the Porsche and drive off.

***

With his eyes glued to his emails on his phone, Trey made his way to the entrance of his gym. Once he entered, the receptionist greeted him with a massive smile,

"Welcome home, Trey." They both laughed, then she watched him make his way to his office. Sensing a presence entering their office, Kaleel looked over his laptop to see Trey standing there smiling.

"Long time man." Trey greeted Kaleel, then walked over to his desk. Kaleel stood up not believing his eyes, then hugged him.

"Damn right, where' you been?" Kaleel stepped back then spotted some scratches on Trey's neck and face. "Ah I see, some wild nights with Chyna, huh?" Trey screwed up his face almost immediately, feeling sick of the thought of it.

"Nah," Trey shook his head then sighed.

Sensing Trey was going to fill him in, he followed him over to Trey's desk and they both sat down. "What happened?" Kaleel asked, getting straight to the point.

"Imagine, I got rid of Chyna." Trey paused, then heard Kaleel sigh. "She's not the one bro," Trey told him.

"What are you on about? Shorty's fine as hell," Kaleel reminded him.

"I know she is, but that's about it."

Disagreeing with Trey, Kaleel replied. "And she's supportive. You're forgetting how hard she worked just to help you open the gym we're in right now."

"And I appreciate that, but she's changed, man! Member the first cheque we cashed? I swear once we got that she changed. I've only just realised it."

"But how has she changed? She seems the same to me."

"Bro, she stopped cooking, she stopped cleaning, she stopped listening to my dreams. All she does now is shop and ask for more money. The money's changed her. She's turned heartless. A few months back, I found out my birth mom died, and when I told her, she told me to move on and to stop thinking about her. She said to focus on Claire cause she's the only one that matters." Trey watched Kaleel gasp and shake his head in disappointment. "Even when I told her about opening the hub, she tried to persuade me not to cause I couldn't profit from it," Trey added, and watched Kaleel's jaw drop to the floor.

"Seriously?"

"Yeah, so I kicked her out of the house, but imagine she let herself back in, trashed the house and set fire to her wedding dress. She even turned up at the hub, smashed all my windows and tried to attack the kids. Oh, and her and Tyanna jumped Ayisha too," Trey added and watched him shake his head in disbelief repeatedly.

"So, she's gone crazy?" Kaleel laughed in shock.

"Mm, I ended up taking back the Porsche and cancelling her credit card."

"Wait, does that mean I can have the Porsche?" Kaleel asked playfully.

"Nah," Trey laughed then offered, "but it's outside if you want to take it for a drive."

"You don't have to ask me twice." Kaleel laughed, then took the keys from Trey.

***

Kaleel rushed over to the Porsche and hopped into the driver's seat. Wasting no time, he turned on the engine and revved it. Trey laughed as he sat down in the passenger's seat. As he watched the doors close themselves, he noticed a police car pulling up with two riot vans following behind. The sound of his phone ringing distracted him from his thoughts. Trey answered to hear Leroy shout,

"Trey!"

"Hey, how's everything?" Trey replied calmly.

"Chyna's gone too far! I had the police searching every single one of my gyms looking for *drugs*. They won't tell me who said there are drugs here, but I know it was Chyna," Leroy said.

Trey sat there holding his phone up against his ear, listening to Leroy and watching the officers rushing towards his gym.

"I've got to go," Trey said, then ended the call.

"What the?" Kaleel muttered, before they both rushed out the car following the officers.

They both re-entered the gym to see police officers scattered everywhere. They're searching everywhere from the gym lockers to their office, to the shower rooms, even the ceilings.

"You can't do that!" The receptionist shouted before she was wheeled away on her chair from her desk. With a serious look on her face, the female officer ignored the receptionist then began to search her desk. She opened each drawer, emptying everything out and then checked her unlocked computer.

"What's going on?" Trey questioned them as he stood there watching helplessly. They ignored him and carried on searching - except one officer. A tall, tanned male with the same physique as Trey. He stepped forward confidently with his chest pushed out arrogantly.

"We've been informed that drugs are being sold here, so we have the right to search the premises." Each word he said angered Trey. He could feel his blood quickly beginning to boil. Not only was he annoyed at the situation, but he also felt disrespected. Trey stepped even closer towards him and replied confidently.

"Well, you won't find any here."

Kaleel stood watching, analysing everything. He knew he had to do something. He could tell from Trey's body language what was about to happen, and he didn't want Trey to do something he'd end up regretting. Not allowing the situation to escalate, Kaleel stepped forward then pulled Trey back. "Just ignore him, he's only built big. We already know they won't find anything anyway." Allowing himself to be pulled away, Trey listened carefully to each word Kaleel had said.

"That's right to listen to your bitch," the office said.

"Look what we have here." Another office shouted, as he exited the ladies' toilets.

"What the heck?" Kaleel mumbled, as he watched the officer walk over to them holding a clear bag with what looked like heroin inside.

Gotta Go!

The officers wasted no time in arresting Trey and Kaleel. They ignored their protests of never seeing the drugs before. The officers enjoyed seeing them panic as they refused Trey and Kaleel their one call. To Trey and Kaleel, it felt like this was personal, and the police were enjoying watching them sweat. Eventually, they were given their call, so Trey called Ayisha and told her everything. She then called Leroy, who spoke to some of his well-respected friends, and within a few hours, Trey and Kaleel were released.

***

As Ayisha drove them home, Trey and Kaleel stared out of the window lost in their thoughts. Everything they had worked so hard for had successfully been targeted and ruined so quickly. Although Trey had grown to dislike Chyna, the more he thought of her, the more he began to despise her – they both did. While driving, Ayisha took a quick glimpse at Kaleel in her mirror. His eyes were red and filled with anger, his lips and eyebrows were tense, and not once did he blink. She then looked over to Trey, who had the same facial expression. Ayisha cleared her throat then addressed Kaleel.

"We're just stopping off at my parent's house first."

***

Trey and Kaleel followed Ayisha into the living room to find Claire, Tanya and Leroy sitting on the sofa.

"Come sit down, son." Claire said to Trey in a fed-up tone of voice. Doing as he was told, Trey walked over to the sofa Claire's was sat on and sat down next to her. He looked around the room at everyone's straight faces, then watched Ayisha and Kaleel sit down too. Claire reached for Trey's hand then held it tight before she cooed. "Son, Chyna's actions are affecting the whole family. Because of her, look where you both ended up." Claire paused, then took a deep breath. "This has gone way too far, and it must stop!"

Tanya nodded then added. "Yes, it's not just between you two anymore, we've all been dragged into this, and it's affecting our businesses and our reputation. We can't have our name attached to drugs." While they spoke to Trey, Kaleel sat on the sofa listening as he composed a bold text. Once it was sent, he looked up from his phone.

"Don't worry, I've had enough of this bitch. She'll be gone today!"

Fearing the worst and knowing what he meant, Claire said, "NO, this will be dealt with the right way! So, you don't have to be looking over your shoulders," Claire paused, then looked at Trey, "so you BOTH can set a good example for those babies over at the hub who look up to you." Knowing exactly what strings to pull, their moods changed quickly. Kaleel nodded with a sombre expression, then decided to send another quick text.

"How do you suggest we do that then?"

Without giving anyone a chance to speak, Leroy made a suggestion. "You need to get a restraining order on her."

"Nar, isn't that what women do?" Kaleel dismissed his suggestion.

Needing to inform, and hopefully persuade them, Claire explained. "No, a restraining order can be filed by a male or a female," Claire paused then said to Trey directly, "a restraining order would keep her away from you, the kids and your business."

Trey nodded. "Mm, but you lot are making her seem like she's dangerous."

Hearing this made Ayisha snap. "Because she is! She is dangerous! You're telling me a woman that would attack kids isn't dangerous? Or set a house on fire isn't? Or plant drugs on you isn't? How did she even find heroin anyway? She's sneaky! There's no telling what she won't do."

"Fair enough, but I won't be getting a restraining order."

"If you won't get a restraining order, then what?" Ayisha asked.

They all sat there thinking in silence, considering all options legally and illegally. "Wait, I know!" Ayisha blurted out with a proud smile on her face.

"What is it?" Trey asked.

Back to normal:

Trey snatched up the bouquet of flowers from the passenger seat then got out of the car. He slammed the door shut, then straightened his freshly ironed white shirt over his dark blue denim jeans. He sighed heavily dreading what was about to happen but headed into the restaurant. Trey followed the waitress over to the table where Chyna was sitting. As Chyna spotted him, she hopped up from her seat like a jack in the box. With a massive smile on her face, she dragged him close to her, wrapped her arms around him and smothered him with kisses. Each kiss he received made his stomach turn. Refusing to ruin the plan, he forced out a smile, stepped out of her hug, then pulled out the flowers that were behind his back. She contained her scream, took the flowers from him, inhaled the sweet aromas, then smiled admiring their beauty. He sat down, watching Chyna and the waitress exchange the flowers for two menus. Chyna looked at him lovingly.

"Baby, I missed you so much." She then stretched out her hand and grabbed his.

He forced out another smile cringing inside then lied, "yeah, me too."

She interrupted him before he could say anything else. "I hated us going back and forth… it was like we were the real-life Mr and Mrs Smith."

"Mm, I hated it too," Trey agreed.

"For a minute I actually thought we were really done." Chyna chuckled. "I knew you'd miss me."

"Mm, I couldn't stop thinking about you," Trey lied again.

"Aww baby, neither could I. But I'm glad we're back together," Chyna said, as she released his hand, then clapped twice grabbing the waiters' attention.

***

The waiter collected their empty starter plates and carried them away. As she sipped on her glass of wine, Chyna asked Trey. "Do you remember how we met?"

"Yeah, I do, at the gym," Trey said bluntly, wondering why she had asked that random question.

"You used to check me out, and I kept wondering when you were going to come and speak to me," Chyna reminded him.

"That's because I wasn't sure if you liked me," Trey confessed.

"How could I not? You were the best-looking guy there. From the way you approached and spoke to me, I knew you were the one and clearly I wasn't wrong."

He nodded then gulped down his lemonade.

Watching him drink, Chyna asked, "Trey, do you remember the day you proposed to me?"

"Yeah, I do," Trey smirked, feeling proud of himself.

"You booked us a holiday and got them to set up a table on the beach." Chyna reminded him with a chuffed smile on her face.

"You know that was their idea, right?" Trey informed her then smiled genuinely. "I told them that I wanted to propose to you, but I didn't know how. It was their idea to put the ring in your glass." The more he spoke about it, the more his heart began to warm up. That day was something he was proud of, and a day he will never forget.

"Aww, I didn't know that. That day was so beautiful... we should go on holiday again," Chyna hinted. Hearing those exact words reminded Trey of the plan.

"Maybe. It won't be any time soon cause we're not back together yet."

"But I thought this meant we are," Chyna said in a disappointed tone.

"Nah, it's gonna take some time for us to get back to how we were before."

***

Trey held the front door open for Chyna then followed her into the house. She made her way through each room, checking to see if anything had been moved or changed. It pained her to know Ayisha had been living in their home and hoped that nothing had been modified.

The kitchen lights flickered on once they sensed a presence. Once the room was fully lit, Chyna made her way over to the wine cabinet. As she made her way over, she touched the surface of the cabinets with the tips of her fingers, absorbing everything. Once she reached the wine cabinet, she opened the doors expecting to see rows of neatly stacked fine wines, but it was empty. Leaning on the door watching her, Trey reminded her.

"You took them all, remember?"

She rolled her eyes regretfully then took a deep breath as she turned around slowly to face him. "I only took them because you don't drink," Chyna said.

Knowing she was lying, but wanting to stick to the plan, Trey nodded then said, "I know you did. They would have just sat there if you didn't take them."

"Exactly." Chyna grinned, then slowly walked over to him, staring deep into his eyes. She leant forward and tried to kiss him as she unbuttoned his shirt, but he stepped back immediately while gently pushing her hands away.

"Not today, Chy. We're working things out." He turned his back to her, then walked into the living room with her following.

"This will fix everything... it'll get us back to normal," Chyna said. Refusing to turn around and look at her, Trey rushed towards the bottom of the stairs as she followed. Once she reached him, she hopped in front of him by standing on the first step, looked down at him and tried again. He stood there watching her unbutton his first, then second, then third button. As each button was undone, the weaker he became. He could feel himself caving in and giving into temptation.

"Stop," he mumbled weakly, then built up enough energy to step away from her. "Not today." Trying his best to stay faithful, he stepped past her then rushed to the room he once shared with her. He let out a sigh of relief once he closed the bathroom door behind him. He sat on the toilet trying his best to remind himself of the plan, but he couldn't help himself. He started to imagine what would've happened if he didn't stop Chyna until he heard movement in his room. He opened the bathroom door to see Chyna crawling on their mattress. He sighed heavily and silently begged God to give him the strength.

"Come join me." Chyna invited him, then tapped the empty space next to her.

"Nah, we won't be sharing the same bed," Trey told her,

"you can sleep here tonight; I'll sleep in the spare room."

"You don't have to!" Chyna said, then got out of the bed and walked over to him seductively. As she made her way over, something caught her eye. "I know that isn't that bitches bag!" Chyna snapped then rushed over to Ayisha's bag that was hanging off the closet door. She picked it up with her fingertips and held it like it was contaminated.

"It is," Trey confirmed, then rushed over and grabbed the bag off her. "If you find any more of her stuff, just put it to the side and I'll drop it off to her."

"Drop it off to her?" Chyna repeated in a confused tone.

"Yeah, we're still on speaking terms... I can't deal with another crazy ex," Trey said sincerely, meaning each word.

"I don't want you speaking to her anymore! I can't stand that hoe and her **perfect self**; she might just suck you back into her trap," Chyna said.

He stood there with Ayisha's bag in his hand, thinking then assured her, "you've got nothing to worry about. You're back where you belong now... pack up anything that belongs to Ayisha then we'll get you some new clothes." Chyna jumped up and down, screaming and clapping excitedly, falling into the bait. She then pulled her phone out of her pocket and rushed over to her closet. She began to record on Snapchat her throwing all Ayisha's stuff carelessly into a bag.

Decisions:

"Chy," Trey called as he entered his room carrying a tray full of food. He watched her stretch under the covers then slowly sit up.

"Aww breakfast in bed," Chyna said, then watched him place the tray on her lap. "I really missed this. It would have been even better if I woke up next to you."

"Mm," Trey said, moved her hair out of her face and kissed her forehead. "So, what have you got planned for today then?" Trey asked, then reached for his phone that was next to her plate.

"Well," she said, then paused to finish what she shoved into her mouth. "I want to get another wedding dress."

"You wouldn't have to if you hadn't burnt the first one."

"I know," Chyna whined, then reassured him before pouting, making the face he once loved, "I won't this time I promise."

"As you're making promises, do you promise not to smash my windows when you get mad? Or not to frame me again and not to try and attack innocent children?" Trey asked, loudly and clearly.

"You're making me sound like some crazy lady," Chyna said with a straight face.

"Well, that's how you were acting… but it's not like I didn't like it," Trey said, then took a piece of toast off her plate. "So, you promise not to do anything like that again?"

"I promise," Chyna said, then winked at him.

"Alright then, shall we go and have a look at some wedding venues instead? You can shop for a wedding dress any day," Trey suggested. She screamed and kicked her legs excitedly, nearly knocking the tray off the bed.

"Are you serious baby?" she asked, without taking her eyes off him.

"Yeah, let's do it right this time. We should even hire a wedding planner."

Unable to contain her excitement anymore, she leant over, grabbed his face and kissed him while feeling the tray slide off her lap. She hopped out of bed, nearly stepping into the splattered food then ran to the door.

"Chy, the food?" Trey called as he watched her.

"Hire a maid, they can clean it up," Chyna said just before she headed to his office to search for wedding venues and planners.

***

Everything seemed to be back to normal. Trey drove while Chyna sat in the passenger seat documenting everything on Snapchat. He looked over at Chyna. "Remember we're dropping Ayisha's stuff off before we get there." Chyna dropped her phone onto her lap then told him,

"Fine, but I'm staying in the car." He took a quick glimpse at the road, then reached for her hand and kissed it.

"Why do you want to stay in the car and hide? I chose you over her, you already know she's got nothing over you. Come show her who she lost to."

Chyna smiled as her confidence skyrocketed. She reached for her handbag to freshen up her makeup.

Trey led the way with Ayisha's stuff in one hand and his keys in the other with Chyna following behind. Each step she took were with her head held high. She swung her hips side to side with her hand firmly on her hip. Shortly after, Ayisha entered the living room to see Chyna and Trey was there.

"Trey?" Ayisha called in shock.

"Hey, I hope you don't mind, the maid let us in," Trey explained.

"Oh… okay," Ayisha said, then walked over to the sofa where her stuff was and looked inside.

"We only came to drop your stuff off," Chyna barked still with her hand on her hip. "He chose me, not you; it's ALWAYS been me, and that's the way it will be."

"Why would he want someone that would try to attack children and frame him?" Ayisha laughed.

"Those kids deserved it and at the time, so did he!" Chyna replied aggressively, then paused, took a deep breath then looked at Trey lovingly, "but we've agreed to forget the past and work it out, right baby?"

"Hell no! No one in their right mind would marry you. I still can't believe I nearly did." Chyna gasped in shock then watched Trey and Ayisha kiss. Seeing their lips connect made her stomach turn.

"What's going on?" Chyna stuttered.

"What? What's going on?" Ayisha mimicked her, "you really are a beauty with no brains. You're out of control, dangerous and you really aren't the one for him."

"Hahaha." Chyna laughed. "You suckers deserve each other, and Trey trust me you're gonna regret this. DEUCES!" Chyna sucked her teeth then tried to march out of the room until Ayisha grabbed her arm.

"No, you don't get to leave, not this time," Ayisha said firmly.

Feeling her arm being grasped, she looked back at Ayisha's hand in disbelief. Chyna yanked her arm out of her grip then pushed Ayisha, watching her stumble back two steps. Before it could escalate any further, Trey rushed in between them and used his arms to push them further away.

"Don't worry Trey I won't hit her," Ayisha said, then calmly sat down on the sofa. Sensing them watching her, Ayisha pulled out her phone and waved it in the air. "Now this can work one of two ways." Ayisha paused, then stopped the recording and played it back loudly addressing Chyna. "Does this sound familiar?"

"So, you recorded me?" Chyna said after listening to the recording. She then started to clap sarcastically.

"We sure did, Trey's even got a recording of you admitting that you had something to do with the drugs at the gym," Ayisha said.

Chyna stood there refusing to say anything. Everything was slowly starting to make sense. Not wanting to show either of them how she was really feeling, she forced out a smile.

"So what? What are you going to do? Call the police?"

"We could do. You already know my dad knows a lot of people, the kind of high-profile people that can release anyone out of jail," Ayisha hinted. "So, what would happen if he gave the police got this recording of you confessing all the crazy stuff you've done... how long do you think you'll get?" Ayisha asked her in a belittling tone. Sensing Chyna wasn't going to answer she guessed, "I don't know, maybe 8, 10, 15 years? But don't worry, I'm sure they'd love you in there."

After swallowing her saliva nervously, Chyna asked, "what would the second option be?"

Immediately, Ayisha looked directly over to Trey and so did Chyna.

"You could leave Houston. We'd give you some money, you take it then travel the world and leave us the hell alone."

Chyna thought about the offer for a few seconds. "If I were to accept this offer, all the recordings would be destroyed, and I'm never to return to Houston again?"

"Yes, or Los Angeles," Ayisha added.

"How much are we talking?" Chyna asked.

"$50,000," Trey told her.

Ayisha corrected him. "$75,000, but you can't come back or contact Trey ever again."

A massive smile grew across Chyna's face as her pupils turned into dollar signs. "That's fine by me, cash or transfer?" Chyna asked with a smug look on her face. Although Trey was the love of her life, there was no way she would turn down the next best thing she loves – money.

"I'll go get the cash-out." Trey told them and pulled the keys out of his pocket.

Chyna blurted out. "I want the Porsche too!"

***

The wait for Trey to return with the cash was more than awkward between Ayisha and Chyna. Ayisha sat on the sofa silently watching Chyna who couldn't keep still. She refused to sit down and avoided eye contact with Ayisha. She was still in disbelief that Trey went behind her back and recorded her without her permission. She was also replaying the moment Trey and Ayisha caught her off guard. The room was utterly silent with only the sound of the clock's ticking being heard. Eventually, the doorbell rang which resulted in Ayisha hopping up. She straightened her top then made her way to let Trey into the mansion.

"Got it?" Ayisha asked nervously.

With a serious expression on his face that showed he meant business, Trey nodded and tapped the black leather suitcase in his hand. He led the way into the living room to see Chyna turn around and face him.

As she walked over to Trey, Chyna asked if it was all there then took the suitcase.

"It's all there," Trey confirmed, then heard Ayisha snigger and throw shade.

"There's no point counting it cause we all know you can't."

Chyna sucked her teeth and ignored Ayisha. She looked at Trey then swallowed her saliva understanding this will be the last time she will see him ever again. She inhaled then exhaled, trying her best to shift the feeling of mourning she felt but she couldn't. Just an hour ago, she was under the impression they were going to plan their wedding, and now she was single again.

Wondering why she was still not leaving, Ayisha questioned her. "What are you waiting for? Hit the road and find yourself a sugar daddy. We both know you'll burn through that money in no time." Chyna looked at Trey then smirked as she thought of the new life she is about to live. She tapped his cheek and felt his soft beard on the palm of her hand for the last time, then made her way to the living room door. She stood in the doorway, took one last look at them then made her way to the car with Trey and Ayisha following.

Outside, Trey and Ayisha stood in front of the mansion door watching her put her suitcase on the passenger seat. Chyna closed the door behind her, then secured herself into the car with her seatbelt. As she did this, she continued to try and shake the feeling of losing Trey off. She looked through the window and watched Ayisha hook her arm onto his which angered her, so she turned on the radio and blasted the music. As she waited for the gates to open, she winded down her window, stuck her hands out and held her middle finger up to them as she exited their lives.

**

Chyna drove along the road singing along to the radio. Although she had just lost the love of her life to Ayisha, she had the Porsche and bundles of money. She looked over at the suitcase full of freshly printed notes and laughed as she wondered where she would travel to first. As she did this, she reached for her phone and unlocked it quickly. She looked up to see the traffic lights had just changed to red. Realising this would be her last time driving around Houston, and with her adrenaline at an all-time high, she pressed harder on the gas and sped through the lights. She laughed as she felt the wind blow through her blue curls, as the Porsche continued to gain speed. With one hand still on the wheel, she opened Snapchat and began to record herself. Looking directly into the camera, Chyna said, "who needs a man when you've got money!" She laughed evilly into her phone then took a quick look at the road. She reached over and opened the suitcase, making it easier for her to record herself touching the money. Once it was opened, she looked up to see that the Porsche was heading towards the other side of the road quickly. She grabbed hold of the wheel and tried her best to steer the car back over while she stamped hard on the brakes. The Porsche span once with the tires screeching before it crashed headfirst into the side of a tow truck.

To be continued...

Part 2 is now available! Search for 'Success with the right queen' on Amazon or head over to www.cassiscreative.com for signed copies

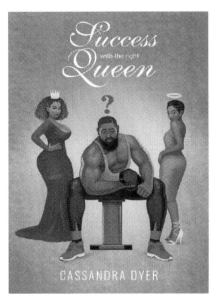

With Chyna finally out of the picture, Trey and Ayisha began to live their lives drama-free, until he received a call that could change everything.

Faced with the fear of possibly losing Chyna forever, Trey's actions cause consequences, despite trying to do the right thing.

A healthy relationship should never crumble, even with a bit of unexpected competition, but everyone has their breaking point, including Ayisha.

Can their relationship make it through this test?

Part 3 is now available! Search for 'Success with my wife to be' on Amazon or head over to www.cassiscreative.com

Apart from love, Trey's life is progressing as planned.
By now, he should be enjoying married life as he envisioned, raising his kids in a loving household, celebrating holidays together and visiting loved ones.

Understandably, being entwined in any love triangle is as chaotic as one could imagine, especially when there are two beautiful and strong women to choose from.
Both ladies have characteristics Trey's looking for in a wife, this makes his decision even more difficult.

Some people would follow their heart, while others would follow their head.

Which lady will Trey meet at the altar?

Thank you for reading my first ever novel, I hope you really enjoyed it. Please feel free to leave an honest review. I also welcome positive criticism.

You can find me on social media:
Instagram: www.instagram.com/Cassiscreative
Personal Instagram: www.instagram.com/Kissandrah
Facebook Reading Group: Keeping Up With Cass The Author
Facebook: www.facebook.com/Cassiscreative

Please be sure to tag us in any selfies or photos to do with this book or send them to us and we will feature you on our pages.
#successwiththewrongqueen #SWTWQ #loveandsuccessseries #cassandradyersbooks

Check out these bookmarks inspired by the 'love and success' series.

Available on my website:

https://cassiscreative.com/collections/bookmarks

or on Etsy:

https://www.etsy.com/uk/shop/Cassiscreative?ref=search_shop_redirect

You'll also find frames, keyrings, journals etc that were also inspired by this series.

Coming soon!

What would you do if you were close to hitting rock bottom, would you exhaust every possible option to better your situation? Or would you accept defeat and throw in the towel?

Meet Pete and Terrence. Both fathers are of a similar age and living in the same city, but their lives are profoundly different.

Though they share the unquestionable love a father has for their child/ren, what challenges await them?
Will they end up making the right decisions or make their situation worse?

I also offer a few design and coaching services.

Head over to

www.cassiscreative.com

for more details.